LION HOUSE Desserts

CHOCOLATE CREAM

CAKE

PAGE 3

Library of Congress Cataloging-in-Publication Data

Davis, Melba.
    Lion House desserts / compiled by Melba Davis.
        p. cm.
    Includes index.
    ISBN 1-57345-625-X
        1. Desserts. I. Title.

    TX773.D296 2000
    641.8'6–dc21   00-021008

Printed in the United States of America   18961-6626

10   9   8   7   6   5   4   3   2

LION HOUSE

Desserts

Compiled by

Melba Davis

EAGLE GATE

SALT LAKE CITY, UTAH

TABLE OF CONTENTS
Desserts

Acknowledgments

Hotel Temple Square Corporation would like to express special appreciation to Melba Davis for her valuable assistance in compiling the book. Much work and coordination went into selecting the recipes, cutting them down to family size proportions, and testing them. We also wish to thank Russell Winegar of Panorama for the photographs and Susan Massey for the food styling. Thanks goes to Deseret Book for the concept, editing, design, and production work that made this book possible.

Introduction

Hotel Temple Square Corporation is pleased to present *Lion House Desserts*.

Favorite recipes have been gathered from the Lion House, the Carriage Court Restaurant, and the Joseph Smith Memorial Building Restaurants and brought together here in one comprehensive cookbook. Together these recipes provide a wide array of desserts for any occasion. Cakes, brownies, tortes, and crisps. Punches, puddings, shakes, and sherbets. English trifle and European cobbler. From traditional fruit cake to trendy black-and-white biscotti, this book includes almost any mouth-watering dessert you can imagine.

Recipes are presented in the following categories: cakes, spoon desserts, pies, cookies and bars, sweet breads, and specialty drinks. Each recipe includes a line indicating which restaurant it was taken from: The Lion House, the Carriage Court, or the Joseph Smith Memorial Building.

The Lion House was built in 1855–56 and remains one of Salt Lake City's most important landmarks. Designed by Truman O. Angell, architect of the Salt Lake City Temple, the Lion House was originally built as a home for Brigham Young. It now serves as the perfect spot for wedding breakfasts, receptions, luncheons, dinners, business meetings, and children's birthday parties. The Lion House Pantry located on the first floor has a cafeteria and bakery where you can eat lunch or order desserts for a special occasion.

The Carriage Court Restaurant is housed in the Inn at Temple Square. Located in the heart of downtown Salt Lake City, the Inn at Temple Square has been authentically restored and offers a place of class and style for meetings, lunches, receptions, and overnight accommodations. The Carriage Court Restaurant offers an attractive menu in posh surroundings for breakfast, lunch, and dinner.

Formerly known as the Hotel Utah, the Joseph Smith Memorial Building has been newly renovated and is a center of hospitality for downtown Salt Lake City. This beautiful building has hosted famous governmental dignitaries and celebrities throughout its history. It is an ideal setting for wedding receptions, banquets, meetings, and parties. The Joseph Smith Memorial Building is home to two of Salt Lake City's most unique restaurants: The Garden and The Roof. The Garden Restaurant features a glass ceiling, terra cotta tile, and fountains that create an airy, atrium-like setting for fine dining. The Roof Restaurant gives a splendid view of the valley while providing a gourmet buffet and delectable desserts.

In the tradition of fine dining and of the other Lion House cookbooks, Hotel Temple Square Corporation hopes you enjoy *Lion House Desserts* and that the many favorite recipes presented here become favorites in your own home.

CHIFFON CAKE.
RECIPE ON PAGE 8.

CHAPTER ONE
Cakes

Chocolate Cream Cake

1 package devil's food cake
  mix

PREPARE AND BAKE CAKE MIX according to package directions, baking in two 9-inch round layers. Cool and then split both layers horizontally. You will only use three of the four rounds of cake (freeze the extra layer for the next time you make the cake). While cake is baking prepare Chocolate Frosting and Stabillized Whipping Cream.

To ASSEMBLE THE CAKE: Place one layer of cake on a serving plate. Put half of the Stabilized Whipping Cream on top of the layer of cake. Spread evenly, being careful to leave about ½ inch border around the edge of the cake with no cream. Then put another layer of cake on top of the cream. Repeat the above steps for a total of five layers—chocolate cake layer, cream layer, chocolate cake layer, cream layer, and chocolate cake layer. Gently push down on the cake to set the layers together. Frost entire cake with Chocolate Frosting. Garnish by sprinkling a few chopped walnuts on the top.

Chocolate Frosting

4 tablespoons cocoa

3 cups powdered sugar

4 tablespoons softened
  butter or margarine

2 to 3 tablespoons milk

1 teaspoon vanilla

MIX COCOA AND POWDERED SUGAR in mixing bowl. Add softened butter, milk, and vanilla. Beat until smooth.

Stabilized Whipping Cream

1 tablespoon unflavored
  gelatin

¼ cup cold water

3 cups heavy whipping cream

¾ cup powdered sugar

1½ teaspoon vanilla

COMBINE GELATIN WITH WATER IN A small saucepan. Let stand until thick. Over low heat, stir constantly until just dissolved. Remove from heat and allow to cool slightly. (It should still be liquid.) Whip the cream, sugar, and vanilla until slightly thick in a large mixing bowl. Turn mixer on low and gradually add the gelatin, then beat on high until the cream is thick.

Stabilized Whipping Cream will hold up for 4 to 5 days without separating. It can also be used to garnish cheesecakes or in any recipe that calls for whipped cream or nondairy whipped topping.

Note: Garnish by sprinkling a few chopped walnuts on top, if desired.

LION HOUSE

Black Devil's Food Cake

⅓ cup shortening

½ cups sugar

3 eggs, well beaten

⅔ cup cocoa

½ cup hot water

2 cups unsifted flour

½ teaspoon salt

1 teaspoon baking soda

1 cup thick sour cream

1 teaspoon vanilla

PREHEAT OVEN TO 350° F. Grease and flour three 8-inch pans or two 9-inch pans. Set aside. In a large mixing bowl cream well the shortening and sugar. Add eggs. In a small bowl beat cocoa with the hot water until smooth. Add to the creamed mixture. In a separate bowl sift together flour, salt, and baking soda. Add to the sugar mixture alternately with the sour cream. Add vanilla and beat the mixture well. Bake for 20 to 30 minutes or until a wooden toothpick inserted in center comes out clean. Remove cake from oven to wire racks. Let cool 10 minutes. Turn from pans and finish cooling on wire racks. Frost with any desired frosting.

LION HOUSE

German Chocolate Cake

1 4-ounce package German's
  sweet chocolate

½ cup boiling water

¾ cup butter or margarine
  or shortening*

1½ cups sugar

4 eggs

1 teaspoon vanilla

2¾ cups sifted cake flour

1 teaspoon soda

1 teaspoon salt

1 cup buttermilk*

PREHEAT OVEN TO 375° F. Line three 9-inch cake pans with wax paper. Set aside. In a medium saucepan, melt chocolate in ½ cup boiling water. Allow to cool slightly. In a large mixing bowl cream butter. Gradually add sugar; continue to beat until mixture is light and fluffy. Add eggs, one at a time, beating well after each addition. Blend in vanilla and melted chocolate. In a separate bowl, sift flour with soda and salt. Alternately add flour mixture and buttermilk to chocolate mixture, beating after each addition until smooth.

Pour mixture into the prepared pans. Bake for 30 to 35 minutes or until cakes test done. Allow cakes to cool in pans 10 minutes, then remove from pans and finish cooling on racks. Peel off wax paper when cakes are cooled, then spread Coconut Pecan Frosting between layers and over top of cake.

Coconut Pecan Frosting

3 egg yolks

1 cup sugar

1 cup evaporated milk

½ cup butter or margarine

1 teaspoon vanilla

1⅓ cups flaked coconut

1 cup pecans, chopped

COMBINE EGG YOLKS, SUGAR, milk, butter, and vanilla in a large saucepan. Cook and stir over medium heat until thickened, about 12 to 15 minutes. Be careful to stir mixture constantly or it will burn. Add coconut and pecans. Beat until thick enough to spread. Makes 3 cups, enough to cover tops of three 8- or 9-inch layers or one 9x13x2-inch cake.

Note: For altitudes of 3,000 to 5,000 feet, increase sugar to 1¾ cups. For altitudes of 5,000 to 7,000 feet, use above recipe.

*If using vegetable shortening, use 1 cup plus 2 tablespoons buttermilk.

LION HOUSE

Quick German Chocolate Cake

1 package white or yellow
    cake mix*
1 package (3 ounces) instant
    chocolate pudding mix*
¼ cup flour
2 cups milk
3 egg whites, beaten stiff

PREHEAT OVEN TO 375° F. Grease and flour a 9x13x2-inch pan. Set aside. Combine cake mix, pudding mix, flour, and milk and beat according to cake package directions. Fold in egg whites. Spoon into prepared pan and bake for 35 to 40 minutes, or until a wooden toothpick inserted in center comes out clean. Frost with Coconut Pecan Frosting (see page 4 for recipe).

A cake mix that already contains pudding mix may be used. Prepare according to package directions.

LION HOUSE

Chocolate Sheet Cake

2 cups flour
2 cups sugar
½ cup butter or margarine,
    softened
½ cup shortening, softened
4 tablespoons cocoa
1 cup water
½ cup buttermilk
1 teaspoon baking soda
1 teaspoon cinnamon
1 teaspoon vanilla
2 eggs, beaten
Dash salt

PREHEAT OVEN TO 400° F. Grease and flour a 10x15-inch jelly-roll pan. Set aside.

In a large bowl, sift together flour and sugar. Set aside. In a medium saucepan, mix together butter, shortening, cocoa, and water and bring to a boil. Pour over flour and sugar mixture. Mix well. Add buttermilk, soda, cinnamon, vanilla, eggs, and salt; mix well. Pour into jelly-roll pan and bake for 20 minutes. Five minutes before cake is done, prepare frosting.

Frosting

½ cup butter or margarine
4 tablespoons cocoa
1 teaspoon vanilla
6 tablespoons milk
4 cups powdered sugar
1 cup chopped nuts

IN A MEDIUM SAUCEPAN MELT butter; add cocoa, vanilla, and milk, and bring to a boil. Remove from heat and add powdered sugar and nuts. Mix well. Frost cake while hot.

LION HOUSE

Old-Fashioned Pound Cake

1 cup butter

2 cups sugar

1 teaspoon vanilla

8 eggs

3¾ cups cake flour

2 tablespoons lemon juice
and zest to taste

Whipped cream (optional)

Strawberries (optional)

PREHEAT OVEN TO 350° F. Grease and flour two 8x4x2½-inch loaf pans. Set aside. In a large mixing bowl, cream butter and sugar until very light. Add alternately vanilla and eggs with cake flour on low speed. Whip on low speed until light and fluffy. Add lemon juice and zest, again beating until light.

Pour into loaf pans and bake for 45 to 60 minutes or until a wooden toothpick inserted into center of cakes comes out clean. Serve with cream and strawberries, if desired. Makes two loaves, 10 to 12 slices.

JOSEPH SMITH BUILDING

Oatmeal Cake

1½ cups boiling water

1 cup rolled oats

½ cup shortening

1 cup brown sugar

1 cup sugar

2 eggs, well beaten

1½ cups flour

1 teaspoon cinnamon

½ teaspoon nutmeg

1 teaspoon soda

½ teaspoon salt

PREHEAT OVEN TO 350° F. Grease and flour a 13x9x2-inch baking pan. Set aside. Pour boiling water over oats in a large mixing bowl and let stand until cool. In a separate bowl, cream shortening with sugars and eggs until fluffy. Add water and oats mixture. Sift together flour, cinnamon, nutmeg, soda, and salt. Sift flour mixture into creamed mixture and blend well. Pour into prepared baking pan. Bake for 35 to 45 minutes or until cake tests done. While cake is baking make topping. Spread topping on baked cake as soon as it comes from oven. Makes 15 servings.

Topping

½ cup butter or margarine

1 cup brown sugar

⅓ cup evaporated milk

1 cup coconut

1 cup nuts, chopped

1 teaspoon vanilla

MELT BUTTER IN A MEDIUM SAUCEPAN and add sugar. Blend. Add remaining ingredients, stir, then spread on baked cake. Place under broiler for a minute or two until the topping is bubbly and golden brown.

LION HOUSE

Brunch Cake Supreme

1 cup butter
1¼ cup sugar
1 egg
⅓ teaspoon vanilla
2 cups cake flour
¼ teaspoon salt
¾ teaspoon baking powder
½ teaspoon soda
1 cup sour cream

PREHEAT OVEN TO 350° F. In large mixing bowl, cream butter and sugar. Add egg and vanilla. In a separate bowl combine flour, salt, baking powder and soda. Alternately add flour mixture and sour cream to creamed mixture.

Spray bundt pan with nonstick cooking spray and layer half the batter on the bottom spreading evenly. Sprinkle with a light layer of topping mixture, then use remaining batter evenly on top of mixture. Top with a light sprinkling of topping mixture. Bake for 40 minutes. This cake is good served warm or cold. Serves 12.

Topping

1½ cups brown sugar
1 scant tablespoon cinnamon
1 cup nuts, chopped

IN MEDIUM BOWL COMBINE brown sugar, cinnamon, and nuts. Store in covered container.

LION HOUSE

Skillet Cake

⅔ cup flour
1 teaspoon baking powder
½ cup butter or margarine
⅔ cup sugar
2 eggs
2 tablespoons milk

PREHEAT OVEN TO 350° F. Line a 9-inch ovenproof skillet with aluminum foil. Grease and flour the foil.

In a small bowl, sift together the flour and baking powder; set aside. In a medium mixer bowl, cream the butter or margarine and gradually add the sugar. Beat until light and fluffy. Add the eggs, one at a time, and beat for 1 minute after each egg. Blend in half of the dry ingredients; then add milk. Blend well, add the remaining dry ingredients, and blend thoroughly. Pour batter into the foil-lined skillet and bake for 25 to 30 minutes, or until cake springs back without leaving an imprint when touched lightly on top. During the last 10 minutes of the cake's cooking time, make topping.

Topping

¼ cup butter
¼ cup sugar
2 tablespoons flour
1 tablespoon cream or evaporated milk
½ cup slivered almonds

COMBINE BUTTER, SUGAR, flour, and cream or evaporated milk in a small saucepan. Cook over medium heat, stirring constantly, until mixture comes to a boil. Spread over hot cake; sprinkle with almonds. Place under broiler for 1 to 3 minutes or until light brown. Serves 8.

LION HOUSE

Chiffon Cake

1¼ cups sugar

3 teaspoons baking powder

2¼ cups cake flour

1 teaspoon salt

½ cup salad oil

5 egg yolks

¾ cup water

2 teaspoons vanilla

2 teaspoons grated lemon
rind (optional)

1 cup egg whites (7 or 8 large
eggs)

½ teaspoon cream of tartar

PREHEAT OVEN TO 325° F. Sift dry ingredients together in a mixing bowl. Add oil, egg yolks, water, vanilla, and lemon rind to the dry ingredients. Beat until smooth. Beat egg whites in a separate bowl with cream of tartar until they form stiff peaks. Pour yolk mixture over whipped whites, folding together until blended. Bake in an ungreased 10-inch tube pan for 55 minutes, then increase temperature to 350° F. and bake for an additional 10 to 15 minutes. When cake tests done, invert the tube pan and let hang until cool. Glaze with Lemon Butter Glaze or Chiffon Cake Frosting, if desired.

LION HOUSE

Lemon Butter Glaze

1½ tablespoons milk

1 tablespoon butter

1¼ cup powdered sugar

1 tablespoon lemon juice

½ teaspoon grated lemon
rind

HEAT MILK AND BUTTER TOGETHER in a small saucepan. Stir in sugar and mix until smooth. Add lemon juice and lemon rind; beat until shiny. Add a drop or two more liquid if needed to make desired consistency. Makes about ½ cup or enough to glaze the top of a cake baked in a 10-inch tube pan, an 8- or 9-inch square pan, or a 9x5x13-inch loaf pan.

Pictured on page viii with Lemon Butter Glaze.

Chiffon Cake Frosting

1 12-ounce carton frozen
whipped topping or
2 recipes Stabilized
Whipping Cream

1 can lemon pie filling

PLACE WHIPPED TOPPING AND PIE FILLING in a bowl and fold together. Slice chiffon cake horizontally in thirds. Place first layer on a plate and spread with a layer of frosting. Add second layer of cake; spread with frosting. Top with third layer of cake. Frost top, sides, and inside circle of cake with frosting. Garnish with lemon twists, if desired.

LION HOUSE

Yvoni's Pineapple Cake

1 yellow (pudding in the mix) cake mix
½ cup cream of coconut
½ cup pineapple juice
4 eggs
⅓ cup oil
½ to ¾ cup crushed pineapple, drained
Fresh strawberries (optional)

PREHEAT OVEN TO 350° F. Grease and flour a 9x13x2-inch cake pan.* Set aside. In a large mixing bowl combine all ingredients except crushed pineapple. Blend well, then fold in pineapple. Place in prepared pan and bake for 40 to 50 minutes. Remove from oven and cool on rack. Serves about 15.

* May be baked in any shaped pan, such as a bundt cake pan or an angel food cake pan.

Note: May be served plain or with 12-ounces whipped topping (or 1 recipe Stabilized Whipping Cream) with fresh strawberries and well-drained pineapple folded in.

LION HOUSE

Pineapple Nut Cake

1 20-ounce can crushed pineapple in juice
2 cups flour
2 cups sugar
2 eggs
2 teaspoons baking soda
1 cup chopped walnuts or pecans

PREHEAT OVEN TO 350° F. Grease and flour a 9x13x2-inch cake pan. In a large bowl, combine pineapple in juice, flour, sugar, eggs, baking soda, and nuts. Mix together until well blended. Pour into the prepared cake pan. Bake for 35 to 45 minutes or until golden brown on top. Remove from oven and allow to cool.

Topping
1 8-ounce package cream cheese, softened
2 cups powdered sugar
½ cup butter or margarine
1 teaspoon vanilla

BLEND CREAM CHEESE, powdered sugar, butter or margarine, and vanilla in a small bowl. Frost cooled cake. Serves 15.

LION HOUSE

Date Picnic Cake

2 cups brown sugar
2 cups walnuts
2 cups chocolate chips
3 cups boiling water
10 ounces dates, chopped
1½ teaspoons soda
1⅓ cups sugar
1½ cups margarine
3 eggs
4¾ cups cake flour
1½ teaspoons salt
1½ teaspoons cinnamon

PREHEAT OVEN TO 350° F. Grease and flour a sheet cake pan; set aside. In a large bowl, mix together brown sugar, walnuts, and chocolate chips to make topping. Set aside.

In a separate bowl, pour boiling water over dates. Stir in the soda, cover, and let rest for 15 minutes. In another mixing bowl, cream sugar and margarine; add eggs and beat well. Add the date mixture and stir. Mix in flour, salt, and cinnamon. Spread on prepared pan. Sprinkle the top with the topping mixture. Bake for 30 minutes or until cake tests done.

Cut into 3x3-inch squares while still warm. Makes 35 squares.

Note: Do not open oven door during baking or cake will fall.

LION HOUSE

Apple Spice Cake

½ cup shortening
1½ cups sugar
1 egg
1½ cups applesauce
2½ cups flour
2 teaspoons soda
½ teaspoon salt
½ teaspoon cinnamon
½ teaspoon cloves
½ teaspoon allspice
½ cup hot water
½ cup nuts
1 cup raisins

PREHEAT OVEN TO 350° F. Grease and flour a 9x13x2-inch cake pan or two 8-inch round pans. Cream shortening and sugar together in a large mixing bowl. Add egg and beat until creamed; add applesauce and mix well. In a separate bowl, sift together the flour, soda, and spices. Add half of the flour mixture and blend in, followed by half of the water. Repeat, adding remaining flour and water. Fold in nuts and raisins. Pour into prepared pan(s) and bake for 45 minutes. Cut into squares. Makes 15 to 20 servings.

JOSEPH SMITH BUILDING

Pumpkin Cake Roll

3 eggs
1 cup sugar
⅔ cup canned or cooked
    pumpkin
1 teaspoon lemon juice
¾ cup flour
1 teaspoon baking powder
2 teaspoons cinnamon
1 teaspoon ginger
½ teaspoon nutmeg
½ teaspoon salt
½ cup chopped nuts
Powdered sugar
¼ cup margarine, softened
2 3-ounce packages cream
    cheese, softened
1 cup powdered sugar
½ teaspoon vanilla

PREHEAT OVEN TO 350° F. Line a 10x15-inch jelly-roll pan with wax paper, and grease paper. Set aside. Beat eggs till lemon colored. Gradually add sugar. Stir in pumpkin and lemon juice. Sift flour, baking powder, cinnamon, ginger, nutmeg, and salt; add to egg-pumpkin mixture. Pour batter into pan; sprinkle with chopped nuts. Bake for 15 minutes. Sprinkle powdered sugar on kitchen towel. Turn cake onto towel, and remove wax paper. Roll up cake and towel lengthwise. Cool. Refrigerate or freeze.

    Whip margarine and cream cheese together. Beat in 1 cup powdered sugar. Add vanilla. Unroll cake and spread with filling. Roll up again. Cut in half. Wrap each roll in plastic wrap until served.

JOSEPH SMITH BUILDING

Carrot Cake

1 cup sugar
½ cup oil
2 eggs, beaten
1½ cups grated carrots
1 cup unsifted flour
½ teaspoon salt
1 teaspoon soda
1 teaspoon cinnamon
¼ cup ground coconut
¼ cup nuts
¼ cup raisins

PREHEAT OVEN TO 400° F. Lightly grease and flour a 9x9-inch square cake pan. Set aside. Combine sugar and oil in a large mixing bowl. Add eggs; mix well. Add grated carrots. Slowly stir in sifted dry ingredients. Add coconut, nuts, and raisins and mix well. Pour batter into prepared pan and bake for 20 to 30 minutes or until cake tests done. When cool, spread with Cream Cheese Frosting.

Cream Cheese Frosting
1 8-ounce package cream
    cheese, softened
¼ cup margarine
2½ cups powdered sugar
Hot water, as needed

CREAM TOGETHER CREAM CHEESE, margarine, and sugar in a mixer bowl. Add a little hot water, one teaspoon at a time, until you reach desired spreading consistency.

LION HOUSE

Lion House Cheesecake

Crust

1½ cups graham cracker
    crumbs, rolled fine
3 tablespoons sugar
6 tablespoons butter or
    margarine

IN A MEDIUM BOWL THOROUGHLY MIX INGREDIENTS. Press firmly into a 10-inch deep dish pie pan or springform pan, lining bottom and sides; set aside. Make filling.

Filling

3 8-ounce packages softened
    cream cheese
1 cup sugar
3 eggs
¾ teaspoon vanilla

IN A LARGE MIXER BOWL BEAT CREAM CHEESE well. Add sugar a little at a time; add eggs one at a time; add vanilla. Combine thoroughly. Pour into crust; fill to within ½ inch of top to allow room for topping. Bake 55 to 60 minutes at 300° F. While cheesecake is baking, prepare topping.

Topping

1 pint sour cream
3 tablespoons sugar
½ teaspoon vanilla

IN A SMALL MIXER BOWL WHIP SOUR CREAM; add sugar gradually; add vanilla. Pour over baked cheesecake and bake at 300° F. for 10 minutes. Allow to cool. Refrigerate until ready to serve. Makes 10 to 12 servings.

LION HOUSE

SPENCER W. KIMBALL'S RASPBERRY
CHEESECAKE. RECIPE ON PAGE 14.

Cheesecake with Shortbread Crust

1½ cups flour

¼ cup sugar

1 egg yolk, lightly beaten

½ cup butter, softened

1 egg white, lightly beaten

2 cups cottage cheese

3 large eggs, separated

½ cup sugar

½ cup sour cream

2 teaspoons cornstarch

1 teaspoon grated lemon
    peel

½ cup chopped walnuts
    (optional)

IN A LARGE BOWL STIR TOGETHER flour and sugar; make a well in the center. Place beaten egg yolk and butter in the well and knead into dry mixture, using your hands, until well blended. Press the dough into the bottom and along the sides of a 9-inch springform pan. Make sure there is a continuous crust all the way around the side of the pan, and make sure the sides meet the bottom crust all the way around. Brush the entire shell with the egg white covering both sides and bottom. (This will seal dough and keep it from becoming soggy.)

Preheat oven to 325° F. Press the cottage cheese through a sieve and drain. In a large bowl, beat the egg yolks until light and foamy; then slowly add the sugar, continuing to beat until smooth and light. Add the cottage cheese to the egg mixture, blending well. Stir in the sour cream, cornstarch, lemon peel, and walnuts. Continue stirring until all ingredients are mixed completely. Beat the egg whites until they form soft peaks, then gently fold them into the batter. Pour the batter into the prepared crust and bake for 1 hour. Cool to room temperature before serving. Serves 16.

LION HOUSE

Spencer W. Kimball's Raspberry Cheesecake

1 3-ounce package lemon
    gelatin

1 cup hot water

1 cup evaporated milk,
    chilled and whipped

1 8-ounce package cream
    cheese, softened

1 cup sugar

1 teaspoons lemon juice

½ cup butter

28 graham crackers, crushed

1 cup whipping cream,
    whipped and sweetened

1 to 2 cups fresh or frozen
    raspberries

IN A MIXER BOWL DISSOLVE GELATIN in hot water; cool and blend in whipped evaporated milk. In a separate bowl, beat cream cheese with sugar. Gently combine gelatin mixture with cream cheese mixture; fold in lemon juice. In another bowl, melt butter and combine with cracker crumbs. Place half of crumbs on bottom of 9x13-inch pan. Pour gelatin/cream cheese mixture on top and sprinkle with remaining crumbs. Chill at least 3 hours to set. Serve with whipped cream and raspberries. Makes 10 to 12 servings.

LION HOUSE

Pictured on page 13.

Easy Cherry Cheesecake

2 cups graham cracker
    crumbs
½ cup melted margarine or
    butter
1 8-ounce package cream
    cheese, softened
2 tablespoons milk
1 cup powdered sugar
½ teaspoon vanilla
2 cups whipped topping
    (1 envelope mix
    prepared by package
    directions)
1 can cherry pie filling

In a 9x13x2-inch pan, mix graham cracker crumbs with melted margarine. Use a fork and level well, then press firmly in bottom and along sides of pan. In a medium bowl, combine and mix the cream cheese, milk, powdered sugar, and vanilla until smooth. Fold in the whipped topping. Spread over cracker crumbs, then cover with chilled cherry pie filling. Chill 2 hours. Makes 18 to 24 servings.

Lion House

Lemon Cheesecake

1½ cups graham cracker
    crumbs, rolled fine
3 tablespoons butter or
    margarine, melted
3 8-ounce packages cream
    cheese, softened
1 cup sugar
3 eggs
¾ teaspoon vanilla
⅓ cup lemon juice
1 pint sour cream
3 tablespoons sugar
½ teaspoon vanilla

Preheat oven to 300° F. Mix together graham cracker crumbs and butter or margarine. Press firmly into bottom and sides of a 9- or 10-inch springform pan.

In a large mixer bowl whip cream cheese; gradually add sugar; then add eggs one at a time. Stir in vanilla. Stir in lemon juice. Pour filling into crust. Bake 60 minutes. Whip sour cream; add sugar and vanilla. Spread on top of cheesecake and return to oven. Bake for 10 more minutes. Cool before removing sides from springform pan. Garnish with lemon zest. Refrigerate until ready to serve. Makes 10 to 12 servings.

Lion House

Pumpkin Cheesecake

1½ cups graham cracker
    crumbs, rolled fine
3 tablespoons butter or
    margarine, melted
3 8-ounce packages cream
    cheese, softened
1 cup sugar
3 eggs
¾ teaspoon vanilla
1⅓ cups plus 2 tablespoons
    pumpkin
¾ teaspoon cinnamon
¼ teaspoon nutmeg
¼ teaspoon ginger
¼ teaspoon cloves
½ teaspoon salt
1 pint sour cream
3 tablespoons sugar
½ teaspoon vanilla

PREHEAT OVEN TO 300° F. Mix together graham cracker crumbs and butter or margarine. Press firmly into the bottom of a 10-inch springform pan.

Whip cream cheese in a mixer bowl; gradually add sugar; then add eggs one at a time. Stir in vanilla. In a separate bowl, combine pumpkin, cinnamon, nutmeg, ginger, cloves, and salt. Mix well, then add to cream cheese mixture. Pour filling into crust. Bake 60 minutes. Whip sour cream; add sugar and vanilla. Spread on top of cheesecake and return to oven. Bake for 10 more minutes. Cool before removing sides from springform pan. Garnish with a sprinkle of nutmeg. Refrigerate until ready to serve. Makes 10 to 12 servings.

LION HOUSE

Chocolate Cheesecake

2 cups Oreo® cookie crumbs,
    rolled fine
3 8-ounce packages cream
    cheese, softened
1 cup sugar
3 eggs
¾ teaspoon vanilla
⅓ cup chocolate syrup
1 pint sour cream
3 tablespoons sugar
½ teaspoon vanilla
Chocolate chips

PREHEAT OVEN TO 300° F. CRUSH WHOLE OREO COOKIES, including frosting centers, to make 2 cups of fine crumbs. Press evenly into the bottom of a 10-inch springform pan.

Whip cream cheese in a mixer bowl; gradually add sugar; then add eggs one at a time. Stir in vanilla. Stir in chocolate syrup. Pour filling into crust. Bake 60 minutes. Whip sour cream; add sugar and vanilla. Spread on top of cheesecake and return to oven. Bake for 10 more minutes. Cool before removing sides from springform pan. Garnish with a few chocolate chips. Refrigerate until ready to serve. Makes 10 to 12 servings.

LION HOUSE

Peppermint Cheesecake

2 cups Oreo® cookie crumbs, rolled fine

3 8-ounce packages cream cheese, softened

1 cup sugar

3 eggs

¾ teaspoon vanilla

1 teaspoon peppermint extract

2 drops red food coloring

1 pint sour cream

3 tablespoons sugar

½ teaspoon vanilla

Peppermint candy, crushed

PREHEAT OVEN TO 300° F. CRUSH WHOLE OREO COOKIES, including frosting centers, to make 2 cups of fine crumbs. Press evenly into the bottom of a 10-inch springform pan.

Whip cream cheese in a mixer bowl; gradually add sugar; then add eggs one at a time. Stir in vanilla, peppermint extract, and red food coloring. Pour filling into crust. Bake 60 minutes. Whip sour cream; add sugar and vanilla. Spread on top of cheesecake and return to oven. Bake for 10 more minutes. Cool before removing sides from springform pan. Garnish with crushed peppermint candy. Refrigerate until ready to serve. Makes 10 to 12 servings.

LION HOUSE

Black Forest Cheesecake

2 cups Oreo® cookie crumbs, rolled fine

3 8-ounce packages cream cheese, softened

1 cup sugar

3 eggs

¾ teaspoon vanilla

1 teaspoon almond extract

⅓ cup maraschino cherry juice

⅓ cup diced maraschino cherries

1 pint sour cream

3 tablespoons sugar

½ teaspoon vanilla

½ cup chocolate chips

PREHEAT OVEN TO 300° F. CRUSH WHOLE OREO COOKIES, including frosting centers, to make 2 cups of fine crumbs. Press evenly into the bottom of a 10-inch springform pan.

Whip cream cheese in a mixer bowl; gradually add sugar; then add eggs one at a time. Stir in vanilla, almond extract, and maraschino cherry juice. Fold in maraschino cherries. Pour filling into crust. Bake 60 minutes. Whip sour cream; add sugar and vanilla. Put ½ of sour cream topping on cheesecake; set remaining half aside. Melt chocolate chips and stir into the remaining sour cream topping. Then swirl this mixture into the topping already on the cheesecake. Return to oven and bake for 10 more minutes. Cool before removing sides from springform pan. Refrigerate until ready to serve. Makes 10 to 12 servings.

LION HOUSE

Orange Slice Cake

2 cups sugar

1 cup butter

4 eggs

½ cup buttermilk

1 teaspoon baking soda

3½ cups sifted flour

½ pound dates, diced

1 pound candied orange
   slices, cut in pieces

1½ cups sweetened, flaked
   coconut

2 cups walnuts or pecans,
   chopped

1 cup orange juice

2 cups powdered sugar

PREHEAT OVEN TO 350° F. Grease a 10-inch tube pan. In a large bowl, cream sugar and butter until light and fluffy. Add the eggs, one at a time, beating well after each addition. In a small bowl, combine buttermilk and baking soda; add to creamed mixture alternately with 3 cups of the flour. Beat well. Dredge dates, candied orange slices, coconut, and nuts in the remaining ½ cup flour. Add to cake batter and mix well. Pour batter into pan and bake for 1 to 1½ hours.

Meanwhile, mix orange juice with powdered sugar. When cake is removed from oven, pour orange juice mixture over the top. Let stand in pan for about 30 minutes. Remove when cool. Refrigerate overnight or longer before serving. The longer this cake sets, the better it tastes. Serves 14.

LION HOUSE

Orange Sponge Cake

8 eggs, separated

¼ teaspoon salt

1 teaspoon cream of tartar

1⅓ cups sugar

Grated rind from one
   orange

¼ cup orange juice

1 cup plus 2 tablespoons
   flour, sifted

½ cup almonds, blanched
   and toasted

1 cup cream, whipped

IN A MIXER BOWL BEAT EGG WHITES and salt until foamy; add cream of tartar and beat until stiff, but not dry. Add ⅔ cup sugar gradually, beating after each addition. In a separate bowl beat egg yolks until very thick and lemon colored; add remaining ⅔ cup sugar, orange rind, and orange juice. Fold the two mixtures together and fold in flour. Bake for 1 hour in an ungreased 10-inch angel cake pan at 325° F. Remove from oven and invert for one hour.

Put almonds through food chopper (or chop coarsely). Spread whipped cream on cake and sprinkle with almonds, or glaze with Orange Butter Glaze.

Orange Butter Glaze

1½ tablespoons milk

1 tablespoon butter

1¼ cups powdered sugar

1 tablespoon orange juice

½ teaspoon grated orange
   rind

HEAT MILK AND BUTTER TOGETHER in a small saucepan. Stir in powdered sugar and mix until smooth. Add orange juice and rind. Beat until shiny. Add a drop or two more liquid if needed to make desired spreading consistency.

LION HOUSE

Coconut Cake

1 cup shortening

2 cups sugar

4 eggs (separated)

½ teaspoon vanilla

½ teaspoon lemon extract

3 cups flour

3 teaspoons baking powder

¼ teaspoon salt

1 cup milk

Coconut Cream Filling

½ cup sugar

⅓ cup flour

¼ teaspoon salt

2 eggs, beaten

1½ cups milk

¾ teaspoon vanilla

3 tablespoons butter or
    margarine

½ cup shredded coconut
    (fresh, frozen, or dried)

Coconut Frosting

1⅔ cups sugar

¼ teaspoon cream of tartar

½ cup water

½ cup egg whites

Shredded coconut

PREHEAT OVEN TO 350° F. Grease and flour three 8-inch round cake pans.

In a large bowl, cream shortening with sugar until light and fluffy. Add egg yolks, vanilla, and lemon extract; beat well. In a separate bowl, sift flour with baking powder and salt and add to creamed mixture alternately with milk, mixing well. In a small bowl, beat egg whites until stiff peaks form. Fold into cake batter. Pour batter into prepared pans. Bake for 25 to 30 minutes. Cool thoroughly.

BLEND SUGAR WITH FLOUR and salt in a medium saucepan. Add eggs and milk. Cook over a low heat, stirring constantly, until mixture thickens. Remove from heat and stir in vanilla, butter or margarine, and coconut. Allow to cool.

Put half of filling on one layer of cooled cake; add the second layer, then the rest of the filling. Top with the third layer of cake. Frost sides and top of cake with Coconut Frosting.

COMBINE SUGAR, CREAM OF TARTAR, and water in a medium saucepan. Cover and heat until mixture boils; remove cover and cook to 260° F. on a candy thermometer. In a small bowl, beat egg whites with electric mixer until stiff peaks form. Pour syrup gradually over beaten egg whites, beating with mixer all the time. Continue beating until fluffy and thick enough to spread. Spread on top and sides of cake. Sprinkle top and sides of cake with coconut. Serves 12.

LION HOUSE

Banana Nut Fudge Cake

1½ cups sugar

½ cup shortening

3 eggs

1 teaspoon almond extract

1 teaspoon vanilla

1½ cups flour

½ cup cocoa

1 teaspoon soda

½ teaspoon salt

½ cup toasted chopped
almonds or pistachios

1½ cups (about 3 medium)
pureed ripe bananas

PREHEAT OVEN TO 350° F. Spray a 12-cup bundt pan with non-stick cooking spray; set aside.

In a large mixing bowl, cream together sugar and shortening. Add eggs, almond extract, and vanilla; beat until fluffy. In a separate bowl, sift together flour, cocoa, soda, and salt. Stir in nuts with flour mixture. Add flour mixture to creamed mixture alternately with pureed bananas, mixing well. Pour batter into prepared pan and bake for 50 minutes or until wooden toothpick inserted in center comes out clean and cake pulls away from sides of pan. Let stand in pan 10 minutes, then remove from pan and place on a wire rack to cool completely. Drizzle with Chocolate Glaze.

Chocolate Glaze

1 cup sifted confectioner's
sugar

2 tablespoons cocoa

2 tablespoons skim milk

½ teaspoon vanilla

IN A SMALL BOWL STIR TOGETHER sifted confectioner's sugar, cocoa, milk, and vanilla until smooth. Add a few drops of milk, if needed, to achieve desired consistency.

LION HOUSE

Chocolate Macaroon Cake

Coconut Mixture

1 egg white (reserve yolk for
    frosting)
½ cup sugar
1 teaspoon vanilla
1 tablespoon all-purpose
    flour
2 cups finely grated coconut

IN A MEDIUM BOWL BEAT EGG white until soft mounds form. Add sugar and vanilla, gradually beating until stiff peaks form. In a separate bowl, mix flour with coconut, then stir slowly into egg white mixture. Set mixture aside.

Batter

¾ cup hot water
½ cup cocoa
3 egg whites
½ cup sugar
½ cup sour cream
1 teaspoon baking soda
1½ cups sugar
½ cup shortening
3 egg yolks
1 teaspoon vanilla
1 teaspoon salt
2 cups flour

PREHEAT OVEN TO 350° F. Grease and flour an angel food cake pan. Set aside. In a small bowl, measure hot water and add cocoa. Stir to dissolve; set aside. In a large mixing bowl, beat egg whites until soft mounds form; gradually add sugar, beating until meringue stands in stiff peaks. Set aside. Place sour cream in a medium bowl and fold the soda into it. The mixture will grow as you stir it. Set aside. In another bowl, beat sugar, shortening, egg yolks, salt, and vanilla until creamy. Add half of the cocoa mixture and beat until creamy (about 4 minutes). Add the flour, sour cream mixture, and remaining cocoa mixture; blend well. Fold in egg white mixture.

    Place one-third of the cake batter in bottom of prepared pan, then crumble half of the coconut mixture on top of batter. Spread half of the remaining cake batter on top of the coconut mixture. Crumble the rest of the coconut mixture on top of the second layer of cake batter, then spread the remaining cake batter on top of the coconut mixture for a total of 5 layers. Bake for 55 to 65 minutes or until cake tests done. Remove from oven and allow to cool until bottom of pan feels slightly warm. To loosen the sides and center, slide a thin knife along the edges and carefully turn upside down. Allow to cool completely; frost with Frosting.

Frosting

1 cup chocolate chips
2 tablespoons butter
1 egg yolk (reserved from
    cake)
¼ cup half-and-half cream
1¾ cup powdered sugar

MELT CHOCOLATE CHIPS AND BUTTER TOGETHER in a small saucepan. Mix together with egg yolk, half-and-half, and powdered sugar. Beat until mixture reaches desired spreading consistency. You may need to add a little more half-and-half to reach proper consistency.

LION HOUSE

Poppy Seed Cake

1 18-ounce package yellow
    cake mix
1 3¼-ounce package instant
    French vanilla pudding mix
4 eggs
1 cup thick sour cream
½ cup water
1 teaspoon rum flavoring
½ cup butter or margarine,
    melted (or use butter-
    flavored shortening)
¼ cup poppy seeds

PREHEAT OVEN TO 350° F. Combine cake and pudding mixes, eggs, sour cream, water, rum flavoring, butter, and poppy seeds in large bowl of electric mixer. Blend well on low speed, then beat at medium speed for 5 minutes.

Pour batter into well-greased and lightly floured bundt cake pan. Bake for 45 minutes, or until wooden toothpick inserted in center comes out clean. Remove from oven and allow to cool in pan for 15 minutes. Remove from pan and place on a wire rack to cool completely. Drizzle with Orange Glaze.

Orange Glaze
2½ cups powdered sugar
⅓ to ½ cup orange juice

MIX TOGETHER POWDERED SUGAR and orange juice until smooth. Put a tablespoon at a time on top of the cake. It should drape down the sides of cake.

LION HOUSE

Sting of the Bee Cake

1 cup butter (no substitutes)
⅔ cup sugar
2 eggs
3 cups sifted flour
3 teaspoons baking powder
1 teaspoon salt
½ cup milk

PREHEAT OVEN TO 375° F. Cream butter; gradually add sugar, creaming well. Beat in eggs, one at a time until light and fluffy. Add sifted dry ingredients alternately with milk. Spoon batter into a well-greased 9-inch springform pan. Make topping.

Topping
½ cup butter
1 cup finely chopped almonds
    (blanched or unblanched)
½ cup sugar
2 tablespoons milk
2 teaspoons vanilla
½ cup raspberry jam

MELT BUTTER; BLEND in chopped almonds, sugar, milk, and vanilla. Bring to a boil. Remove from heat and allow to cool slightly. Spread carefully over batter. Bake cake for 50 minutes. Remove from oven and cool. Remove sides from springform pan. Prepare Butter Cream Filling.

Split cake horizontally into two layers. Spread bottom layer with Butter Cream Filling; spread raspberry jam over top. Very carefully replace top layer of cake. Cut vertically into thin slices and serve. Makes 16 to 20 servings.

Butter Cream Filling
1 cup butter
2 egg yolks
2 cups powdered sugar
2 teaspoons vanilla

SOFTEN BUTTER. Beat in egg yolks, powdered sugar, and vanilla.

LION HOUSE

Strawberry-Filled Cake

4 eggs
1 cup sugar
1 teaspoon vanilla
¾ cup flour
¼ cup cornstarch
1½ teaspoons baking powder
¼ teaspoon salt

PREHEAT OVEN TO 350° F. Grease and flour an 8-inch round springform pan. Beat eggs until light and fluffy. Add sugar gradually, beating until thick. Add vanilla. Sift flour with cornstarch, baking powder, and salt and fold carefully into egg mixture. Pour into prepared pan and bake for 30 minutes. Cool and remove from pan. Split into three layers.

Filling

1 quart strawberries, mashed
1 cup sugar
1 pint whipping cream,
   whipped and sweetened

MIX MASHED STRAWBERRIES with sugar. Whip the cream and sweeten to taste. Place the first layer of the cake on a serving plate. Spread ⅓ of strawberries on layer. Spread about ¼ of the whipped cream on top of the berries. Repeat with second layer. Spread the rest of the strawberries on third layer, then frost the whole cake with the rest of the whipped cream. Chill until serving; refrigerate any leftovers. Serves 12.

LION HOUSE

Pudding Cake

1 cup finely chopped dates
1 cup finely chopped nuts
½ teaspoon baking soda
1 cup boiling water
1 cup shortening or butter
2½ cups sugar
4 eggs, beaten
1 teaspoon vanilla
3 cups sifted flour
1 teaspoon salt
1 teaspoon baking powder
1 cup orange juice
Ice cream or whipped cream
   (optional)

PREHEAT OVEN TO 325° F. Grease a 10-inch tube pan. In a medium bowl, combine dates and nuts and sprinkle baking soda over them. Add boiling water, stir, and let set. In a separate bowl, cream together shortening or butter and 1¾ cups of the sugar until fluffy. Add eggs and vanilla and beat well. Sift flour, salt, and baking powder together. Add to creamed mixture. Stir in date mixture. Mix well. Pour into prepared pan and bake for 1½ hours. Remove from pan. Mix remaining ¾ cup sugar with orange juice. Pour over hot cake. Serve with ice cream or whipped cream, if desired. Serves 12.

LION HOUSE

Chocolate Decadence

2½ cups semisweet
    chocolate chips
1⅓ cups butter
1 cup (about 12) egg yolks
1½ tablespoons cake flour
1½ tablespoons sugar
⅛ teaspoon cream of tartar
1½ cups egg whites
Raspberry jam or pureed
    raspberries

Preheat oven to 425° F. Grease and flour two 8-inch round pans. Set aside. In a double boiler melt chocolate chips and butter. Cool slightly. In a medium mixing bowl beat egg yolks with flour, sugar, and cream of tartar until mixture turns a lemon color and is thick and creamy. Fold mixture into melted chocolate mixture. Set aside. In a separate bowl whip egg whites until stiff. Fold into cooled chocolate mixture. Pour into prepared pans and bake for 15 minutes exactly. Cake will be soft and loose. Cool. (Do not invert cake to cool.) Frost with raspberry jam that has been thinned with water or with fresh raspberries that have been pureed. Makes 10 to 12 servings.

JOSEPH SMITH BUILDING

Fudge Ribbon Cake

1 package chocolate cake mix
4 ounces cream cheese
1 tablespoon butter
1 extra small egg
½ tablespoon cornstarch
1 teaspoon vanilla
7 ounces or ½ can sweetened
    condensed milk

PREHEAT OVEN TO 300° F. Make cake mix according to directions; fill two 9-inch greased and floured cake pans ⅓ full. Set aside. Blend cream cheese and butter in a small mixing bowl until smooth and creamy. Mix egg, cornstarch, and vanilla and add to cream cheese mixture. Add milk and beat for one minute. Pour half of cream cheese mixture over cake batter in each pan and bake 45 to 60 minutes or until cake tests done. Frost with Chocolate Cream Frosting.

Chocolate Cream Frosting
½ cup plus 4 tablespoons
    butter
½ cup plus 1 tablespoon
    shortening
3 tablespoons cocoa
4⅔ cups powdered sugar
1½ teaspoons vanilla
¼ cup plus 1½ teaspoons
    water

IN A LARGE MIXER BOWL ADD BUTTER, shortening, cocoa, and powdered sugar. Beat until very creamy. Add vanilla and mix until well blended. Add water and mix until very light.

CARRIAGE COURT

Double Decadent Brownie Torte

½ cup butter

½ cup light corn syrup

1 cup semisweet chocolate
chips

½ cup sugar

3 eggs

1 teaspoon vanilla

1 cup all-purpose flour

1 cup walnuts or pecans

PREHEAT OVEN TO 350° F. Grease and flour one 8-inch cake pan. Set aside. In a medium saucepan, put butter, corn syrup, and chocolate chips. Cook on low heat, stirring often, until chips are melted. In a medium mixing bowl whip sugar, eggs, and vanilla together until fluffy. Add flour to sugar mixture and blend well. Add nuts and mix until well blended. Pour into prepared pan and bake 35 minutes. Makes 8 to 10 servings.

JOSEPH SMITH BUILDING

Toffee Torte

1 package devil's food cake
mix

1 16-ounce carton frozen
whipped topping*

7 English toffee bars (Heath®
or Skor®), crushed

GREASE AND FLOUR two 9-inch round cake pans. Prepare and bake the cake according to package directions. Cool on a wire rack. (If time permits the cakes can be frozen for easier handling.) Carefully cut each layer horizontally to make 2 layers. Place thawed whipped topping in a bowl and fold in 6 of the crushed candy bars. Place one layer of the cake on a serving plate and spread with topping mixture. Repeat with the remaining 3 layers. Frost the sides and top with the topping mixture. Sprinkle the remaining crushed bar on top of the cake.

*A double recipe of Stabilized Whipping Cream may be substituted for the frozen whipped topping. See recipe on page 3.

LION HOUSE

Coconut Torte

1 cup sugar

4 tablespoons instant starch

2 20-ounce cans crushed
   pineapple

1 drop yellow food coloring

1 white or yellow cake mix

12-ounces frozen whipped
   topping or a double
   recipe of Stabilized
   Whipping Cream

2 cups coconut

IN A MEDIUM BOWL MIX SUGAR and starch together. Pour pine-apple, undrained, on top of the mixture. Add food coloring, then stir until blended. (There will be little white lumps in this mixture that will dissolve as it sits.) Set aside in refrigerator overnight.

Grease and flour two 9-inch round cake pans. Set aside. Prepare and bake cake according to package directions. Allow to cool on wire racks.

Slice cakes in half horizontally. Place first layer of cake on a serving plate and spread ⅓ of the pineapple filling on top. Place next layer of cake on top and spread with whipped topping, about ¼ inch thick. Place third layer of cake on top and spread with half of remaining filling. Top with last layer of cake. Frost top and sides of entire cake with whipped topping. Cover sides of cake with coconut. Top with remaining pine-apple filling and a sprinkle of coconut. Makes 12 to 14 servings.

Note: The pineapple filling for this cake should be made a day ahead. This recipe can also be made using canned lemon, blueberry, or cherry pie filling.

LION HOUSE

Strawberry Angel Torte

4 egg whites

¼ teaspoon salt

¼ teaspoon cream of tartar

1 cup sugar

1 cup heavy cream, whipped

1 quart fresh strawberries
   (washed, hulled, and
   halved) or 1 10-ounce
   package frozen
   strawberries (drained)

1 tablespoon powdered sugar

PREHEAT OVEN TO 275° F. Butter a 9-inch pie pan. Set aside. To make torte shell, place egg whites, salt, and cream of tartar in a small bowl. Beat at high speed until eggs are frothy and begin to stiffen. Add sugar gradually and beat to very stiff peaks (8 to 10 minutes). Spread meringue in prepared pie pan. Bake until dry, about 1 hour.

To make filling, spread one-half of whipped cream in the torte shell. Put shell in refrigerator and let it stand five hours or overnight. If using fresh strawberries, toss with powdered sugar and spoon into torte shell. Top with remaining whipped cream. If using frozen strawberries, fold into remaining whipped cream and pile into torte shell. Drizzle with juice drained from frozen berries. Serve.

LION HOUSE

Peppermint Torte

Devil's food cake mix

¼ cup finely crushed peppermint candies

½ bag (10½ ounces) mini marshmallows

1 cup walnuts, chopped

2 12-ounce containers of whipped topping

15 to 20 Starlight mints

½ package chocolate sandwich cookies, rolled into crumbs

PREPARE DEVIL'S FOOD CAKE MIX according to package directions and bake in two greased and floured 9-inch round layers. Allow to cool; slice each layer in half to make 4 thin layers. Place a piece of wax paper between each layer and put sliced cake in the freezer while you make the filling.

To make filling, mix together in a large mixing bowl peppermint candies, marshmallows, nuts, and 1 container whipped topping. Mix until smooth. This should set for at least 30 minutes before using; chilling in the refrigerator for 2 or 3 hours is recommended. Remove cake layers from the freezer and separate the layers. Spread ⅓ of the peppermint filling on the first layer; then place another layer of cake on top of the filling. Repeat this process with the next 2 layers. Place the last layer on top and frost the sides and top with the second container of whipped topping. Take a handful of cookie crumbs and gently pat on to side of cake. Repeat until sides of cake are covered with crumbs. Garnish with rosettes of whipped topping, starlight mints, and cookie crumbs.

LION HOUSE

Peppermint Angel Food Dessert

1 angel food cake

¾ cup crushed red and white peppermint stick candy

½ cup milk

1½ teaspoons unflavored gelatin (½ envelope)

2 teaspoons water

1 pint whipping cream, whipped until stiff

½ cup chocolate syrup

SLICE ANGEL FOOD CAKE INTO 3 horizontal layers and set aside. Put candy and milk in a small saucepan; heat and stir until candy is dissolved. In a small bowl soften gelatin in water, then add to milk and candy mixture. Chill until it starts to set. Fold into whipped cream.

Place one layer of cake on a serving plate. Spread about ⅓ of cream mixture over bottom layer of cake. Drizzle chocolate syrup over whipped cream mixture. Place another layer of cake and repeat. Repeat with third layer. Cover outside of cake with remaining whipped cream mixture. Chill and serve. Makes 12 servings.

LION HOUSE

Caramel Pudding Cake

4 cups water

2 cups brown sugar

¼ cup plus 4 tablespoons
    butter or margarine

1 cup sugar

1 cup peeled apples, chopped

2 cups flour

1 teaspoon nutmeg

1 teaspoon cinnamon

2½ teaspoons baking powder

½ teaspoon salt

1½ teaspoon baking soda

1 cup milk

1 teaspoon vanilla

1 cup raisins

½ cup chopped nuts

Whipped topping (optional)

PREHEAT OVEN TO 375° F. GREASE A 13x9x2-inch cake pan. Set aside. In a large saucepan mix and boil together water, brown sugar, and 4 tablespoons butter. Set aside.

In a large mixer bowl cream ¼ cup butter. Add sugar and cream together thoroughly. Add chopped apples. Sift dry ingredients together and add alternately with milk. Stir in vanilla, raisins, and nuts. Spread batter into prepared pan. Pour hot brown sugar mixture over batter. Bake for 45 minutes. Cut in squares and serve, warm or cold, with whipped topping, if desired. Makes 20 to 24 servings.

LION HOUSE

Luscious Lemon Cake

1 package white cake mix

1 cup water

¼ cup sugar

2 eggs, beaten

2 tablespoons cornstarch

2 tablespoons sugar

Zest of 1 lemon

1 tablespoon butter

3 tablespoons lemon juice
    (fresh)

1 pint sweetened whipping
    cream

¼ cup white chocolate
    shavings

GREASE AND FLOUR TWO 9-INCH cake pans. Set aside. Preheat oven and make cake according to package directions on cake mix. When cake is done, put on cake racks and cool completely. (Cake may be frozen for future use.) While cake is cooling, prepare lemon filling.

Put water, ¼ cup sugar, and beaten eggs in a small saucepan. Mix cornstarch and 2 tablespoons sugar together in a small bowl. Slowly add to mixture in pan. Cook on medium heat, stirring constantly until thickened. When thickened, add lemon zest, butter, and lemon juice. Stir until butter is melted and mixture is well mixed and smooth. Remove from heat and let cool. Cover with plastic wrap while cooling.

When cake is cool, cut each layer in half to make 4 slices. Place a layer on a serving plate and spread with ½ of cooled lemon filling. Add second layer of cake and spread with whipped cream. Add third layer of cake and spread with the remaining half of lemon filling. Top with forth layer of cake. Frost sides and top of cake with whipped cream. Garnish with white chocolate shavings. Refrigerate until ready to serve. Serves 12 to 16.

CARRIAGE COURT

Angel Food Cake

1 cup plus 2 tablespoons
    sifted cake flour
1½ cups sifted sugar
1¼ cups (10 to 12) egg
    whites, at room
    temperature
¼ teaspoon salt
1¼ teaspoons cream of
    tartar
1 teaspoon vanilla
¼ teaspoon almond extract

Preheat oven to 375° F. In a medium bowl, sift flour and ½ cup sugar together. Set aside. Combine egg whites, salt, cream of tartar, and flavorings in large bowl. Beat with flat wire whip, sturdy egg beater, or at high speed of electric mixer until soft peaks form. Add remaining 1 cup sugar gradually, ¼ cup at a time, beating well after each addition. When beating by hand, beat 25 strokes after each addition. Sift in flour mixture in four additions, folding in with 15 fold-over strokes each time and turning bowl frequently. (Do not stir or beat.) After last addition, use 10 to 20 extra folding strokes.

Pour batter into ungreased 9- or 10-inch tube pan. Bake 35 to 40 minutes for 9-inch cake and 30 to 35 minutes for 10-inch cake, or until cake springs back when pressed lightly. Cool cake in pan, upside down, 1 to 2 hours. Then loosen from sides and center of tube with knife and gently pull out cake. (An angel cake pan with a removable bottom is ideal for removing cake in perfect condition.)

Lion House

Angel Fluff

1 small (9-ounce) angel food
    cake
1 cup half-and-half cream
1 cup whipping cream, stiffly
    beaten
1 cup sugar
⅓ cup lemon juice

In large serving bowl (2-quart) break cake into bite-size pieces. In small bowl of electric mixer or with hand electric mixer, gradually beat half-and-half into whipped cream. The result will be a fluffy, thick liquid. Beat sugar into mixture, adding it gradually, then add lemon juice slowly, still beating. Pour this mixture over cake pieces. Chill for at least 2 hours. Spoon onto dessert plates and serve with Pineapple Sauce. Makes 8 servings.

Pineapple Sauce

4 tablespoons cornstarch
1 cup sugar
2 cups pineapple juice
½ cup lemon juice

Combine cornstarch and sugar and mix well in a small saucepan. Add pineapple juice and cook on medium heat, stirring constantly, until clear and thickened, about 5 minutes. Add lemon juice. Remove from heat. Chill.

Lion House

Chocolate Custard. Recipe on page 33.

CHAPTER TWO
Spoon Desserts

Chocolate Custard

2 eggs
¾ cup egg yolks
1½ cups cream
¾ cup milk
7 ounces dark chocolate
    (bitter or semisweet)
¾ cup sugar

IN A MEDIUM MIXING BOWL whip whole eggs, yolks, and sugar together. Set aside. Scald milk and cream in medium saucepan. Add chocolate to milk and cream and stir until melted. Slowly add egg mixture to hot chocolate milk, stirring constantly. Pour into ramkins or custard cups and bake in a water bath for 25 to 30 minutes at 350° F. Serves 6 to 8 depending on size of cups.

Pictured on page 30.

JOSEPH SMITH BUILDING

Chocolate Brownie Pudding

2 cups all-purpose flour
2 teaspoons baking powder
1½ cups sugar
¼ cup cocoa
1 teaspoon salt
1 cup milk
2 teaspoons vanilla
¼ cup butter, melted
1½ cups walnuts, chopped
1½ cups brown sugar
½ cup cocoa
3½ cups hot water

PREHEAT OVEN TO 350° F. GREASE A 9x13x2-inch pan and set aside. Measure flour, baking powder, sugar, ¼ cup cocoa, and salt into a bowl and mix together. Add milk, vanilla, and melted butter and mix until incorporated. (This can be mixed by hand or with the mixer.) Stir in the walnuts. Pour into prepared pan and set aside.

    In a large bowl mix together brown sugar and ½ cup cocoa. Pour hot water over sugar and cocoa mixture and mix together. When well blended, slowly pour over the flour mixture in baking pan. (The baking pan will be very full, so handle carefully when putting it in the oven.) Bake for 35 to 40 minutes. Cut into 15 squares.

LION HOUSE

Chocolate Pudding Dessert

1½ cups flour
¾ cup butter
⅔ cup chopped nuts
1 cup powdered sugar
1 8-ounce package cream
    cheese, softened
1 9-ounce carton frozen
    whipped topping
2 3-ounce packages instant
    chocolate pudding
3 cups milk

PREHEAT OVEN TO 325° F. IN A medium bowl combine flour, butter, and nuts and cut together as for pie crust, until they resemble coarse meal. Press well into a 9x13x2-inch baking pan. Bake for 30 minutes. Remove from oven and cool.

In a mixer bowl beat together sugar and cream cheese until fluffy. Add ½ of the whipped topping. Spread on cooled crust.

In another bowl make up pudding according to package directions, using 3 cups milk. Spread pudding on cream cheese layer. Spread remaining whipped topping on pudding layer. Sprinkle with additional chopped nuts, if desired. Chill several hours or overnight. Makes 15 servings.

Note: Butterscotch or other instant pudding flavors may also be used.

LION HOUSE

Chocolate Cream

4 egg yolks
8 ounces sweet cooking
    chocolate, coarsely
    chopped
½ cup butter or margarine
4 egg whites
2 tablespoons sugar
Finely chopped orange peel
    (optional)
Whipped cream (optional)

IN A SMALL BOWL BEAT EGG YOLKS until lemony in color. Set aside. Place chocolate and butter or margarine in a small, heavy saucepan. Heat over low heat, stirring constantly, until melted. Gradually stir about half the chocolate mixture into the beaten egg yolks. Return all to saucepan and continue cooking and stirring over low heat for an additional 2 minutes or until very thick and glossy. Remove from heat and let cool to room temperature.

In a mixer bowl beat egg whites until soft peaks form. Gradually add sugar, continuing to beat until stiff peaks form. Fold a small amount of the egg whites into chocolate mixture to lighten it; then fold the chocolate into the remaining beaten egg whites. Spoon mixture into dessert glasses by quarter-cupfuls. Cover and place in refrigerator for several hours or overnight. Garnish with chopped orange peel or whipped cream, if desired. Serves 10.

LION HOUSE

Creamy Vanilla Pudding

2 cups milk (2%)
¼ cup sugar
2 tablespoons cornstarch
¼ teaspoon salt
1 teaspoon vanilla

Heat milk in the top of a double boiler until very hot. Combine sugar, cornstarch, and salt in a small bowl and stir in ½ cup of the hot milk. Stir until sugar is dissolved. Add sugar mixture slowly to the hot milk in double boiler, stirring constantly. Cook and stir until mixture thickens and is smooth, about 3 minutes. Cover and cook 5 minutes longer. Remove from heat and stir in vanilla. Cover with plastic wrap and let stand until cool. Refrigerate for 3 hours before serving. Makes 4 servings of pudding, or fills one batch of cream puffs or eclairs, or makes one 9-inch pie.

Lion House

Tapioca Pudding

3 cups milk
⅓ cup plus 1 tablespoon sugar
1 egg, slightly beaten
3 tablespoons minute tapioca
Pinch salt
1 teaspoon vanilla

Heat 2½ cups milk and 1 tablespoon sugar in top pan of a double boiler until skim forms and milk is scalded. In a medium bowl beat eggs slightly and add tapioca, ⅓ cup sugar, salt, and the reserved ½ cup milk and whisk together. Pour this mixture very slowly into the scalded milk, stirring constantly. Stir for 1 minute and again every 2 minutes for the next 4 minutes. (Mixture will form a ball of tapioca on the bottom if not stirred enough; this ball can be stirred out, but pudding will not be as smooth and creamy.) Allow to cook 2 to 4 more minutes. Tapioca will swell and begin to turn clear. Turn off heat and allow pudding to sit over the hot water about 20 minutes. Add vanilla. Stir, then remove top pan from water. Serve warm or place in serving dishes and chill. Makes 6 servings.

Note: Pudding can be made in a saucepan on the stove instead of in a double boiler but it must be stirred constantly and removed from heat when the tapioca has swelled and turned clear. Cool 5 to 10 minutes before dishing.

Lion House

Steamed Carrot Pudding

1 cup carrots, grated

¾ cup raw potatoes, grated

½ cup apples, grated*

½ cup salad oil

1 cup raisins

½ cup walnuts or pecans

1 cup sugar

1 cup flour

1 teaspoon cinnamon

½ teaspoon allspice

½ teaspoon cloves

½ teaspoon nutmeg

½ teaspoon salt

1 teaspoon soda

COMBINE CARROTS, POTATOES, APPLES, oil, raisins, and nuts in mixing bowl and mix with a spoon until blended. In a separate bowl mix sugar, flour, cinnamon, allspice, cloves, nutmeg, salt, and soda. Add flour mixture to carrot mixture and stir until blended. It will form a stiff, gooey mixture.

Place mixture in a clean, greased number 2 can or in an ovenproof bowl of about the same size. Do not fill container more than ¾ full. Cover container with foil. Cook the pudding in a pressure cooker or steam it.

To PRESSURE COOK: Place rack in bottom of cooker to keep pudding from touching the bottom. Add about ¾ inch water; set container of pudding in cooker. Cook 20 minutes with the steam valve open, and then an additional 50 minutes with the valve closed.

To STEAM: Place container of pudding in a pot that is tall enough to fit the container and still have a tight lid on. Add about 1 inch water. Place lid on tightly and cook for 2½ hours.

The pudding can be made ahead of time and stored in the refrigerator. Warm in the oven or microwave before serving. Serve topped with Lemon Sauce.

Lemon Sauce

1 cup sugar

2 tablespoons cornstarch

2 cups cool water

¼ cup lemon juice

2 tablespoons butter

COMBINE SUGAR, CORNSTARCH, AND water in a saucepan. Heat to boiling, stirring constantly. Add lemon juice and butter.

*With or without peel

LION HOUSE

Rice Pudding

2 cups milk

1 small can (5⅓ ounces) evaporated milk

½ cup plus 2 tablespoons sugar

2 eggs, slightly beaten

¼ teaspoon salt

1 tablespoon cornstarch

2 cups cooked rice

½ cup raisins

⅛ teaspoon nutmeg

⅛ teaspoon cinnamon

1 teaspoon vanilla

Place 1½ cups of the milk plus the can of evaporated milk and 6 tablespoons sugar in the top of a double boiler. Heat together until milk is scalded. In a mixing bowl, whisk eggs together until they are broken apart. Add salt and the remaining 4 tablespoons sugar to the eggs and whisk again. Slowly pour egg mixture into scalded milk, stirring constantly with a wire whisk. Allow to cook 15 to 20 minutes, stirring occasionally. In a small bowl mix reserved ½ cup milk and cornstarch together and slowly pour into milk mixture, stirring constantly until pudding begins to thicken. (Be careful to stir constantly or lumps will form.) Stir thoroughly and allow to cook 10 to 15 more minutes or until cornstarch flavor is gone. Add cooked rice, then allow pudding to cook 7 more minutes. Remove from heat and add raisins, nutmeg, cinnamon, and vanilla. Serves 8.

Note: If a double boiler is not available, you can place a stainless steel bowl on top of a small saucepan of boiling water, or pudding can be made in a saucepan, but it will need constant care and stirring. It will not need to cook as long if made in a saucepan.

Lion House

Hotel Utah Rice Pudding

½ cup rice

1 cup water

1 quart whole milk

1 vanilla bean, split

3 eggs, whole

½ cup sugar

¼ to ½ cup golden raisins, as desired

In a small saucepan cook rice in 1 cup water until it is slightly undercooked. Drain. Add milk and vanilla bean. Bring milk just to a boil. (Watch carefully that milk does not come to an actual boil.) In a bowl, blend eggs and sugar together, then add to milk, stirring constantly. Cook on low heat until pudding thickens. Be careful not to overcook or pudding will curdle. Take off heat and add raisins. Pudding will thicken more as it cools. Serves 6.

Joseph Smith Building

Christmas Pudding

2½ cups all-purpose flour
1¼ cups granulated sugar
2½ teaspoons nutmeg
½ teaspoon cloves
1 teaspoon salt
2½ teaspoons cinnamon
2½ teaspoons soda
1¼ cups brown sugar
2½ cups apples, grated
2½ cups carrots, grated
2½ cups potatoes, grated
2½ cups raisins (seedless)
1⅓ cups dates, chopped
1 cup maraschino cherries,
　chopped
1¾ cups butter, melted
1⅓ cups nuts, chopped

IN A LARGE MIXING BOWL MEASURE flour, granulated sugar, nutmeg, cloves, salt, cinnamon, and soda. Mix together so that the spices are well distributed. Add to this mixture the brown sugar, apples, carrots, potatoes, raisins, dates, cherries, butter, and nuts. Mix on low speed until well blended. Put mixture into 7 wide-mouth pint jars which have been sprayed with nonstick spray.* Cover the top of each jar with 2 layers of plastic wrap. Then cover with a piece of foil and put a rubber band around the foil. Steam for 4 hours. When it is done, refrigerate until cool. Take off plastic wrap and foil. Clean edges of jar and put on new plastic, foil, and rubber band. Pudding will keep for months if it is kept cold. Serve with Butterscotch Sauce if desired. Makes 30 servings.

You can use different size cans or containers as desired, as long as they are sprayed with nonstick spray.

Butterscotch Sauce

1½ cups brown sugar
⅔ cup light corn syrup
½ cup water
Dash salt
⅔ cup evaporated milk

COMBINE BROWN SUGAR, CORN SYRUP, water, and salt in a small saucepan. Heat to boiling, stirring until sugar is dissolved. Continue cooking until a small amount dropped in cold water forms a very soft ball. Remove from heat. Cool slightly, then stir in evaporated milk. Makes 2 cups sauce.

Pictured on page 39.

LION HOUSE

Heber J. Grant's Fig Pudding

2 pounds white dried figs
8 cups soft bread crumbs
4 cups brown sugar
1 cup white sugar
1 pound ground suet
3 tablespoons molasses
4 tablespoons flour
3 teaspoons grated nutmeg
Juice of 4 lemons
8 eggs

GRIND FIGS IN MEAT GRINDER. Mix with all other ingredients, except eggs, in a large bowl. Beat egg yolks and egg whites separately. Stir yolks into fig mixture, then fold in whites. Thoroughly grease five 1-pound cans and fill ⅔ full. Steam for 3 hours. If pudding is made ahead, let cool completely and then refrigerate.

Source: Frances Grant Bennett, daughter of President Heber J. Grant.

LION HOUSE

CHRISTMAS PUDDING. RECIPE ON PAGE 38.

Baked Apple Pudding

4 cups apples, chopped
(canned or fresh)

2 cups sugar

2 eggs

½ cup butter

1 cup raisins

1 cup nuts, chopped

2 cups all-purpose flour

2 teaspoons soda

1 teaspoon salt

½ teaspoon nutmeg

2 teaspoons cinnamon

Vanilla Sauce

2 cups sugar

2 cups brown sugar

¼ cup cornstarch

1 cup butter

1 teaspoon vanilla

4 cups water

PREHEAT OVEN TO 350° F. Grease and flour a 9x13x2-inch dripper pan or cake pan. Set aside. Chop apples. In a large bowl, place chopped apples; stir in sugar, then add eggs. Cut butter into small pieces and add to mixture. Stir together well. Add raisins and nuts; stir. In a separate bowl, mix together flour, soda, salt, nutmeg, and cinnamon. Add to apple mixture; stir together well. Put in prepared pan. Bake for 40 to 50 minutes. Cake can be served hot or cold. Cut into squares and serve each piece topped with hot Vanilla Sauce. Makes 15 to 18 servings. (This recipe makes a lot, but will keep well.)

IN A SAUCEPAN COMBINE SUGAR, brown sugar, cornstarch, butter, vanilla, and water. Cook and stir over medium heat until thickened. The sauce is best served hot. This makes more than enough but will keep well.

LION HOUSE

Plum Pudding

1½ cups chopped, pitted
    prunes
½ cup orange juice
1 medium apple, peeled and
    grated
¾ cup chopped walnuts
½ cup mixed candied fruits
1 tablespoon grated orange
    peel
½ cup butter, softened
1½ cups brown sugar
3 eggs
3 cups flour
1 teaspoon cinnamon
½ teaspoon baking soda
½ teaspoon salt
½ teaspoon ginger
½ teaspoon nutmeg
1¼ cups milk

Orange Sauce

¾ cup butter
1¼ cups powdered sugar
3 tablespoons orange juice
½ teaspoon vanilla

To MAKE PUDDING: In a medium bowl, soak prunes in orange juice for 1 hour. Stir in grated apple, walnuts, candied fruits, and orange peel. In a large mixer bowl, cream butter; add brown sugar and beat well. Add eggs one at a time and beat until fluffy. Sift together flour, cinnamon, baking soda, salt, ginger, and nutmeg. Add dry ingredients to creamed mixture alternately with milk and mix well. Stir in prune mixture. Grease and flour 1 large or 2 or 3 medium molds or cans. Spoon mixture into containers about ⅔ full. Cover with foil. Place containers on rack in large kettle with 2 inches of water. Steam 2 hours for large or 1½ hours for smaller containers, or until toothpick inserted near center comes out clean. Cool 15 minutes and invert on wire rack.

To MAKE SAUCE: In a small mixer bowl, beat butter and powdered sugar together until fluffy. Add orange juice and vanilla and beat well.

To serve: Spoon warm pudding into dessert dishes and top with sauce. Pudding and sauce can be stored in refrigerator up to two weeks. Wrap pudding in plastic wrap and foil. To reheat, return pudding to original mold and steam for 30 to 40 minutes. Serves 18.

LION HOUSE

Baked Custard

4 eggs, slightly beaten
2¾ cups milk
½ cup table cream
½ cup sugar
½ teaspoon salt
¾ teaspoon vanilla
Nutmeg (optional)

IN A MEDIUM BOWL BEAT EGGS; ADD milk, cream, sugar, salt, and vanilla. Strain into individual custard cups set into a pan of hot water. Sprinkle nutmeg on custard, if desired. Bake at 350° F. for 40 to 50 minutes. Custard is done when knife inserted near center comes out clean. Remove from water to cool. Chill and serve in cups. Makes 6 to 8 servings.

Note: Custard may be baked in a 1½- or 2-quart casserole instead of in individual cups.

LION HOUSE

Flan

1 14-ounce can sweetened condensed milk
1 12-ounce can evaporated milk
4 ounces cream cheese (optional)
3 eggs
1 tablespoon vanilla
1 cup sugar

IN A BLENDER, COMBINE CONDENSED milk, evaporated milk, cream cheese (if desired), eggs, and vanilla and blend until well mixed. Sprinkle sugar over the bottom of a heavy frying pan. Place over low heat and cook, stirring constantly, until sugar melts and starts to turn golden brown. (Watch carefully; sugar burns easily at this point.) Pour caramelized sugar into an 8-inch round cake pan, tilting pan to coat bottom completely. Carefully pour the mixture from the blender over the sugar. Place the pan in a larger dish or baking pan and fill the larger pan with water to a depth of 1 to 2 inches. Bake at 300° F. for 35 to 50 minutes or until the sides are firm and top is lightly browned. Let cool and flip pan upside down on a plate to serve. Serves 6.

LION HOUSE

Bread Pudding

10 slices bread*

Approximately 1 cube
    butter, melted

¾ to 1 cup raisins

6 eggs

6 cups milk

¾ cup sugar

Pinch salt

¾ teaspoon vanilla

¾ teaspoon plus dash
    nutmeg

PREHEAT OVEN TO 350° F. Spray a 9x13-inch pan with non-stick spray and set aside. Cut crusts off bread. Place one layer of bread slices in pan and brush with melted butter. Sprinkle raisins on top. Place another layer of bread on top of raisins and brush with melted butter.

In a large bowl, mix eggs, milk, sugar, salt, vanilla, and ¾ teaspoon nutmeg with a wire whisk. Pour this mixture over the bread. Sprinkle a little nutmeg over the top of the pudding and allow to set for 30 to 45 minutes. Bake for 45 minutes or until custard is formed and a knife inserted comes out clean. Serve with Lemon Butter Sauce. Serves 16.

*Stale bread can be used for this recipe.

Lemon Butter Sauce

2 cups sugar

¼ cup plus ½ teaspoon
    cornstarch

¼ teaspoon salt

2 cups water

1 cup butter, cut in small
    pieces

1½ teaspoons lemon extract

PUT SUGAR, CORNSTARCH, and salt in a 4-quart saucepan. Stir until blended. Add water. Bring to a boil and cook for 5 minutes, stirring constantly. Remove from heat and stir in butter and lemon extract. Stir until butter is melted and mixture is creamy. Pour a small amount on each piece of bread pudding. Makes 4 cups.

Note: This sauce is delicious and can be used on other puddings and cakes.

LION HOUSE

Marbled Caramel Surprise Pudding

2½ cups water

1 cup brown sugar

2 tablespoons butter

1 cup flour

2 teaspoons baking powder

½ teaspoon salt

¼ cup vegetable shortening

1 cup brown sugar

1 cup raisins

1 cup chopped walnuts

½ cup milk

1 teaspoon vanilla

Half-and-half or ice cream

PREHEAT OVEN TO 350° F. IN a medium saucepan, bring water, 1 cup brown sugar, and butter to a boil. Boil, stirring occasionally, for 5 minutes. Pour sauce into an 8-inch square baking dish. In a medium mixing bowl, stir together flour, baking powder, and salt. Cut in shortening with a pastry blender. Add 1 cup brown sugar, raisins, walnuts, milk, and vanilla; mix just enough to form a sticky batter. Spoon batter into hot sauce in baking dish by rounded tablespoonfuls. It will spread and sink into sauce as it cooks. Bake in preheated oven for

45 minutes. Serve warm with half-and-half or ice cream. Serves 6.

LION HOUSE

Apple Bread Pudding

3 slices whole-grain bread,
    cut into 1-inch cubes

1 apple, peeled, cored, and
    chopped

2 tablespoons raisins or
    chopped prunes

1 can (12 ounces) evaporated
    skim milk

5 egg whites

2 whole eggs

2 tablespoons sugar

½ teaspoon cinnamon

⅛ teaspoon nutmeg

Nutmeg Sauce

⅔ cup sugar

1½ tablespoons cornstarch

⅛ teaspoon salt

1 cup boiling water

4 tablespoons butter-
    flavored granules

½ teaspoon nutmeg

PREHEAT OVEN TO 325° F. SPRAY A 9-inch square baking dish with nonstick cooking spray. Arrange bread cubes, chopped apple, and raisins or prunes in bottom of dish.

In a medium mixing bowl, combine milk, egg whites, whole eggs, sugar, cinnamon, and nutmeg. Beat with an electric mixer on medium speed until well mixed. Pour over bread and fruits in baking dish; let stand for 10 minutes. Cover with foil and bake for 20 minutes. Remove foil and bake for 20 to 25 minutes more, or until a knife inserted in center of pudding comes out clean. Place dish on wire rack to cool slightly. Serve pudding warm with Nutmeg Sauce. Makes 6 servings.

IN A MEDIUM SAUCEPAN, COMBINE sugar, cornstarch, and salt. Gradually stir in boiling water. Add butter-flavored granules. Cook and stir over medium heat until mixture is thick and bubbly; continue cooking, stirring constantly, 2 minutes more. Remove from heat. Stir in nutmeg. Serve warm. Makes about 8 servings, 2 tablespoons each.

LION HOUSE

Apple Dumplings

1 quart cooking apples,
　　pared, cored, sliced
　　(about 4 medium apples)
2 tablespoons sugar
2 tablespoons water
1 tablespoon lemon juice

PREHEAT OVEN TO 350° F. IN A large bowl mix ingredients well and place in an 8x8x2-inch baking pan. Cover pan with aluminum foil and bake at 350° F. for 10 to 15 minutes while preparing dough. Remove apples from oven and cover with dough. Cut steam vents in dough. Pour sauce over dough. Return to oven and bake 30 minutes more, or until brown. Serve warm with hot Vanilla Sauce. Makes 9 servings.

Dough
1½ cups flour
¼ cup sugar
¼ teaspoon salt
2 teaspoons baking powder
½ cup vegetable shortening
1 egg, slightly beaten
⅓ cup milk

SIFT DRY INGREDIENTS TOGETHER in a large bowl. Cut in shortening as for pie crust, until mixture resembles coarse meal. In a separate bowl combine egg and milk, then stir into dry ingredients. Combine thoroughly, then knead on lightly floured board about 20 times. Pat and roll out to about ½-inch thickness. Carefully place over apples. Trim excess, if necessary, so that dough fits pan.

Sauce
½ cup brown sugar
⅓ cup water
1 tablespoon butter or
　　margarine
Cinnamon

COMBINE BROWN SUGAR, WATER, and butter in a small saucepan. Boil until sugar is dissolved. Pour over dough. Sprinkle lightly with cinnamon.

Vanilla Sauce
2 tablespoons flour
2 tablespoons sugar
⅛ teaspoon salt
¾ cup hot water
¾ cup evaporated milk (one
　　small can)
½ teaspoon vanilla
2 tablespoons butter or
　　margarine

COMBINE DRY INGREDIENTS in a medium saucepan. Stir in hot water and bring mixture to a boil, stirring constantly. Add evaporated milk, vanilla, and butter. Reheat. Makes about 1½ cups.

LION HOUSE

Zina's Caramel Dumplings

2 tablespoons butter

1½ cups brown sugar

1½ cups water

1¼ cups flour

½ cup sugar

2 teaspoons baking powder

½ teaspoon salt

½ cup milk

1 teaspoon vanilla

Whipped cream or ice cream
(optional)

To make caramel sauce, combine butter, brown sugar, and water in saucepan. Bring to boil; reduce heat to simmer. To make dumplings mix flour, sugar, baking powder, and salt in bowl; stir in milk and vanilla (batter should be stiff). Drop by teaspoonfuls into simmering caramel sauce. Cover pan and simmer for 20 minutes. Do not remove lid till time is up. Spoon into serving dishes and serve with cream or ice cream, if desired. Makes 6 servings.

Lion House

Apple Cranberry Dumplings

2 cups sugar

2 cups water

½ teaspoon cinnamon

½ teaspoon cloves

½ cup butter

2 cups sifted flour

2 tablespoons sugar

1 tablespoon baking powder

1 teaspoon salt

½ cup shortening

¾ cup milk

4 cups grated, peeled apples

1 cup cooked, drained whole
cranberries or 1 cup
whole cranberry sauce

½ cup chopped black wal-
nuts (regular walnuts
may be substituted)

Whipped cream or vanilla
ice cream (optional)

Preheat oven to 425° F. In a medium saucepan, combine 2 cups sugar, water, cinnamon, and cloves. Bring to a boil; boil 5 minutes. Remove from heat and stir in butter. Set aside.

In a medium bowl, sift together flour, 2 tablespoons sugar, baking powder, and salt. Cut in shortening with a pastry blender until mixture is crumbly. Gradually add the milk, tossing the mixture to make a soft dough. Roll dough out on a floured surface to form an 18x12-inch rectangle. Spread the apples, cranberries, and nuts over the dough. Roll up like a jelly roll and cut into 1-inch slices. Lay slices in a 13x9-inch baking dish. Pour the hot syrup over the slices and bake for 40 minutes. Serve warm with whipped cream or vanilla ice cream, if desired. Serves 18.

Lion House

Chocolate and Fresh Fruit Trifle

1 angel food cake or 9-inch
    long cake
1 3½-ounce package instant
    chocolate fudge pudding
    mix
2 cups skim milk
1 teaspoon vanilla
2 cups assorted sliced fresh
    fruit: bananas, nec-
    tarines, peaches,
    pineapple, strawberries,
    raspberries, or other
    choices
1 cup light whipped topping
1 tablespoon grated choco-
    late
1 tablespoon sliced almonds

CUT CAKE IN ¾-INCH CUBES. Place half the cubes in the bottom of a large clear glass bowl. Prepare pudding as directed on package, using 2 cups of skim milk. Stir in vanilla. Spoon half of pudding on top of cake cubes; arrange half of fruit on top of pudding. Repeat layers, ending with fruit. Top with whipped topping. Cover and refrigerate until thoroughly chilled, at least 1 hour. Just before serving, top with grated chocolate and slivered almonds. Makes 16 servings.

LION HOUSE

English Trifle

2 to 3 cups stale sponge cake
    or vanilla wafers
1 16-ounce can fruit cocktail
    (or any kind of fruit)
1 3-ounce package gelatin
    (strawberry, raspberry,
    or cherry)
1 3-ounce package instant
    vanilla pudding*
2 cups cold milk
2 cups whipping cream
Chopped nuts
Grated chocolate
Maraschino cherries

LINE BOTTOM OF GLASS SERVING bowl with pieces of sponge cake or vanilla wafers. Drain fruit and arrange over cake. Make gelatin according to package directions, and while still warm, pour over the cake and fruit. Allow to set. Make vanilla pudding by beating pudding powder into cold milk. Pour over set gelatin. Cover with plastic wrap and refrigerate. When ready to serve, whip cream and spread over top of pudding. Decorate with chopped nuts, grated chocolate, and maraschino cherries. Makes 8 to 10 servings.

For a true English trifle, use Bird's Custard powder, which is available at many food stores in gourmet or imported-foods sections. Prepare according to directions on package.

LION HOUSE

European Blueberry Cobbler

1½ cups fresh or frozen
    blueberries
1 teaspoon sugar
⅔ cup skim milk
⅓ cup flour
1 egg
2 tablespoons sugar
1 teaspoon finely shredded
    orange peel
2 teaspoons vanilla
¼ teaspoon cinnamon
1 teaspoon sugar

PREHEAT OVEN TO 350° F. SPRAY A 1½-quart shallow baking dish with nonstick cooking spray; set aside.

Mix blueberries with 1 teaspoon sugar in a medium bowl. Let stand, uncovered, at room temperature for 30 minutes.

Combine milk, flour, egg, 2 tablespoons sugar, orange peel, vanilla, and cinnamon in the container of an electric blender or food processor. Mix until smooth.

Arrange blueberries evenly in the bottom of prepared baking dish. Pour batter over the top, then sprinkle with 1 teaspoon sugar. Bake for 1 hour or until golden brown. Makes 4 servings.

LION HOUSE

Crepes with Strawberries

2 eggs
½ cup flour
1 tablespoon sugar
½ cup milk
2 tablespoons water
1½ teaspoons melted butter
3 cups fresh sliced
    strawberries
⅓ cup sugar
1 cup cottage cheese
1 cup sour cream
½ cup powdered sugar

IN A SMALL BOWL, BEAT EGGS; slowly add flour and 1 tablespoon sugar alternately with milk and water. Whisk or beat with an electric mixer until smooth. Beat in melted butter. Put in refrigerator and chill at least 1 hour. Lightly grease a crepe pan or a medium frying pan. Heat the pan over medium heat for several seconds, lift it off the burner, and pour in 2 or 3 tablespoons of batter. Quickly swirl the pan to cover the bottom with a thin, even layer of batter. Set the pan back on the heat and cook the crepe until the bottom is browned. Carefully flip over the crepe with a spatula. Brown the other side, then remove crepe from pan with a spatula. Repeat until all batter is used.

Combine strawberries and ⅓ cup sugar in a large bowl. Set aside. Using a blender or electric mixer, blend the cottage cheese until smooth. Add sour cream and powdered sugar and stir well. Put a small amount of fruit down the center of a crepe and top with a spoonful of the creamy mixture. Fold one side of the crepe over the filling and roll it up the rest of the way. Repeat with remaining crepes, using about ⅔ of the strawberries. Top with remaining fruit and sprinkle with additional powdered sugar, if desired. Makes 6 servings (2 crepes each).

LION HOUSE

Pavlova

3 egg whites

1½ cups sugar

1½ teaspoons vanilla

1½ teaspoons vinegar or
    lemon juice

¼ cup boiling water

1 cup whipping cream

½ teaspoon vanilla

Sliced fresh fruit: peaches,
    strawberries, bananas,
    kiwi, pineapple

PREHEAT OVEN TO 450° F. BRING EGG whites to room temperature. Line a baking sheet with foil. Using an 8-inch round cake pan as a guide, draw a circle on the foil.

In a large electric mixer bowl, beat together egg whites, sugar, 1½ teaspoons vanilla, vinegar or lemon juice, and boiling water. Beat on high speed for about 12 minutes, scraping bowl constantly, until stiff peaks form and mixture holds its shape but is not dry. Spread the mixture onto the circle on the baking tray. Shape into a pie-shell form with a spoon, making the bottom ½ inch thick and the sides 2½ to 3 inches high. Form the edges into peaks or make a rim around the edge. Place baking sheet in center of preheated oven and turn oven off. Let stand 4 to 5 hours. Do not open oven door.

To serve: Remove meringue shell from foil and place on a serving plate. Whip cream with ½ teaspoon vanilla until soft peaks form; spread in shell, reserving ½ cup for garnish. Arrange sliced fruit on top of whipped cream and add the ½ cup reserved whipped cream in the center of the fruit. Cut and serve immediately. Serves 8 to 10.

LION HOUSE

Raspberry Crunch

2 cups crushed pretzels

3 tablespoons sugar

½ cup margarine or butter

1 8-ounce package cream
    cheese, softened

1 cup sugar

1 12-ounce carton whipped
    topping

1 16-ounce can crushed
    pineapple, drained

1 6-ounce package raspberry
    gelatin

3 cups boiling water

1 10-ounce package frozen
    raspberries

Whipped cream

PREHEAT OVEN TO 400° F. CRUSH pretzels with rolling pin. Mix with sugar and melted butter. Press into bottom of 9x13-inch baking pan. Bake 5 minutes. Cool. Beat cream cheese and sugar till fluffy. Mix in whipped topping. Fold in drained pineapple. Spread mixture onto cooled pretzel crust. Dissolve gelatin in boiling water. Mix in frozen raspberries. Place gelatin in refrigerator till syrupy. Pour over cream cheese layer. Refrigerate till set. Garnish with whipped cream. Makes 12 servings.

LION HOUSE

Cranberry Crunch

½ quart (about ½ pound)
    tart apples, pared,
    cored, and sliced
2 to 3 cups raw cranberries
½ cup water
2 tablespoons butter or
    margarine, melted
½ teaspoon salt
1½ tablespoons cinnamon
1 tablespoon lemon juice
½ cup butter or margarine
1 cup sugar
3 tablespoons flour
1¼ cups crushed corn flakes
    or bran flakes*
Table cream (optional)

PLACE APPLES AND CRANBERRIES IN a 2- or 3-quart baking dish. Combine water, melted butter, salt, cinnamon, and lemon juice. Pour over fruit. In mixing bowl cream together butter and sugar; add flour and mix well. Crush cereal and add to creamed mixture. Press mixture over fruit. Bake, uncovered, at 375° F. for 30 to 35 minutes. Serve with table cream, if desired. Makes 6 to 8 servings.

Raisin Bran® is a good alternate.

LION HOUSE

Pistachio Crunch

1 cup margarine
½ cup brown sugar
2 cups flour
1 cup walnuts, chopped
2 8-ounce packages cream
    cheese
2 cups powdered sugar
2 cups Dream Whip®
2 large 10-ounce packages
    pistachio pudding mix
5⅓ cups milk
Whipped topping
Maraschino cherries

PREHEAT OVEN TO 325° F. IN A LARGE mixing bowl, cream together margarine and brown sugar. Mix in flour and nuts. Press into a 9x13-inch dripper pan and bake for 15 minutes or until lightly browned.

In a separate bowl, beat cream cheese to soften. Add powdered sugar and cream together until smooth. Whip Dream Whip according to package directions and fold into cream cheese mixture. Spread mixture over top of cooled crust and chill for 20 to 30 minutes.

Mix together pudding mix and milk. Whisk with a wire whisk until mix is dissolved. Allow to thicken slightly. Pour pudding mixture on top of chilled cream cheese mixture. Chill until firm. Cut in 24 pieces. Garnish with whipped topping and a cherry. Serves 15 to 18.

LION HOUSE

Chocolate Crunch

1 cup margarine
½ cup brown sugar
2 cups flour
1 cup walnuts, chopped
2 8-ounce packages cream
    cheese
2 cups powdered sugar
2 cups Dream Whip®
2 5½-ounce instant packages
    chocolate pudding mix
5⅓ cups milk
Whipped topping
Maraschino cherry

PREHEAT OVEN TO 325° F. IN A LARGE mixing bowl, cream together margarine and brown sugar. Mix in flour and nuts. Press into a 9x13-inch dripper pan and bake for 15 minutes or until lightly browned.

In a separate bowl, beat cream cheese to soften. Add powdered sugar and cream together until smooth. Whip Dream Whip according to package directions and fold into cream cheese mixture. Spread mixture over top of cooled crust and chill for 20 to 30 minutes.

Mix together pudding mix and milk in a large bowl. Whisk with a wire whisk until mix is dissolved. Allow to thicken slightly. Pour pudding mixture on top of chilled cream cheese mixture. Chill until firm. Cut in 24 pieces. Garnish with whipped topping and a cherry.

LION HOUSE

Apple Crunch

1 quart (about 1 pound) tart
    apples, pared, cored,
    and sliced
½ cup water
2 tablespoons butter or
    margarine, melted
½ teaspoon salt
1½ tablespoons cinnamon
1 tablespoon lemon juice
½ cup butter or margarine
1 cup sugar
3 tablespoons flour
1¼ cups crushed corn flakes
    or bran flakes*
Table cream (optional)

PLACE APPLES IN A 2- OR 3-QUART baking dish. Combine water, melted butter, salt, cinnamon, and lemon juice. Pour over apples. In mixing bowl cream together butter and sugar; add flour and mix well. Crush cereal and add to creamed mixture. Press mixture over apples. Bake, uncovered, at 375° F. for 30 to 35 minutes. Serve with table cream, if desired. Makes 6 to 8 servings.

Raisin Bran® is a good alternate.

LION HOUSE

Apple Crisp

Topping

1 cup butter, cold
1 cup brown sugar
1 cup flour
1 cup oatmeal
¼ teaspoon baking powder

In a large bowl mix together butter, brown sugar, flour, oatmeal, and baking powder just until the butter is broken up and ingredients are mixed. Mixture should be crumbly. Set aside.

Filling

6 cups canned apples or 6 to
    8 fresh apples, peeled
    and sliced
½ cup sugar
¼ teaspoon salt
1 teaspoon cinnamon

Place apples in a 9x13-inch pan. Sprinkle with sugar, salt, and cinnamon. Then crumble crisp topping on top. Bake at 350° F. for 25 to 35 minutes or until golden brown. (If fresh apples are used, bake for 45 minutes.) Serve warm or cold, with whipped cream or ice cream. Makes 12 to 15 servings.

Lion House

Peach Crisp

Topping

1 cup butter, cold
1 cup brown sugar
1 cup flour
1 cup oatmeal
¼ teaspoon baking powder

In a large bowl mix together butter, brown sugar, flour, oatmeal, and baking powder just until the butter is broken up and ingredients are mixed. Mixture should be crumbly. Set aside.

Filling

½ teaspoon cinnamon
¼ cup brown sugar
2 tablespoons cornstarch
2 30-ounce cans sliced
    peaches, slightly drained
1 teaspoon lemon juice

In a small bowl mix together cinnamon, brown sugar, and cornstarch. Set aside. In a large bowl, combine peaches and lemon juice. Stir in cinnamon and sugar mixture. Place in a 9x13-inch pan. Crumble crisp topping on top. Bake at 350° F. for 25 to 30 minutes or until golden brown. Serve warm or cold, with whipped cream or ice cream. Makes 12 to 15 servings.

Lion House

Rhubarb Crisp

Topping

1 cup butter, cold
1 cup brown sugar
1 cup flour
1 cup oatmeal
¼ teaspoon baking powder

IN A LARGE BOWL MIX TOGETHER butter, brown sugar, flour, oatmeal, and baking powder just until the butter is broken up and ingredients are mixed. Mixture should be crumbly. Set aside.

Filling

4 cups rhubarb (frozen, partially thawed)
1¾ cups sugar
¼ cup all-purpose flour
2 tablespoons instant starch or quick gel
¼ teaspoon salt
1 egg
1 drop red food coloring

PLACE RHUBARB IN BOWL and let thaw for 10 to 15 minutes. Drain liquid. In a separate bowl, combine sugar, flour, starch, and salt. Beat egg, then blend with the flour mixture. Add rhubarb and red food coloring. Mix well. Pour into a 9x13-inch pan and crumble crisp topping on top. Bake at 350° F. for 55 minutes or until golden brown. Serve warm or cold, with whipped cream or ice cream. Makes 12 to 15 servings.

LION HOUSE

David O. McKay's Baked Apples

6 apples
¾ cup brown, white, or maple sugar
Lemon juice
Cinnamon
Butter
Cream

PREHEAT OVEN TO 375° F. Wash and core apples. Fill center of each apple with 1 tablespoon sugar, sprinkling a little over the outside. Then sprinkle with lemon juice and cinnamon, and dot with butter. Place in deep casserole with a lid. Add enough water to cover bottom of baking dish. Cover and bake about 35 minutes or until tender. Remove apples and boil syrup remaining in the casserole dish until thick. Pour syrup and thick cream over apples to serve. (If apples are baked uncovered, it is necessary to baste them during cooking.) Makes 6 servings.

Source: Emma Rae McKay Ashton, daughter of President David O. McKay.

LION HOUSE

Winter Pears with Raspberry Sauce

1 3-ounce package cream
    cheese, softened
¼ cup ricotta cheese
2 tablespoons finely chopped
    pecans
4 fresh medium pears
1½ cups fresh or frozen
    raspberries
3 tablespoons water
1 tablespoon sugar
1 teaspoon cornstarch

COMBINE SOFTENED CREAM CHEESE, ricotta cheese, and pecans in a mixing bowl. Wash pears; pat dry. Core each of the pears, leaving a center hole about 1 inch in diameter. Fill each pear center with the cream cheese mixture. Chill. Make sauce by pressing raspberries through a sieve to remove seeds. Combine raspberries and juice with water, sugar, and cornstarch. Cook and stir till thickened. Chill. To serve, cut pears crosswise into ¼-inch slices. For each serving, spoon a little sauce onto dessert plate and place 4 to 5 pear slices on top of sauce. Makes 6 servings.

LION HOUSE

Baked Pears with Caramel Sauce

6 ripe pears
3 tablespoons finely chopped
    pecans
½ teaspoon grated lemon
    peel
¼ cup firmly packed brown
    sugar
3 tablespoons dark corn
    syrup
¼ cup water
1 teaspoon butter or
    margarine

PREHEAT OVEN TO 350° F. CORE PEARS from the bottom, leaving stem ends intact. Mix pecans and lemon peel; pack mixture evenly into centers of pears. Arrange pears, stem ends up, in an ungreased 3-quart baking dish. Add water to a depth of 1 inch. Cover and bake for 50 minutes or until pears are tender.

In a small saucepan, combine brown sugar, corn syrup, ¼ cup water, and butter or margarine. Bring to a boil, stirring constantly until sugar is dissolved. Boil gently, stirring frequently, for an additional 5 minutes. Place warm pears in individual dessert dishes and pour sauce over the tops. Makes 6 servings.

LION HOUSE

Prune Whip

¼ cup sugar

3 tablespoons cornstarch

⅛ teaspoon salt

3 egg yolks

2 cups milk

½ teaspoon vanilla

1 quart small blue prune
   plums

3 egg whites

3 tablespoons sugar

1 teaspoon vanilla

½ cup chopped walnuts

MIX TOGETHER ¼ CUP SUGAR, cornstarch, and salt; set aside. Beat egg yolks until lemony in color. In a medium saucepan, scald the milk over low heat. Do not boil. Add the sugar mixture slowly to the scalded milk, stirring constantly until mixture is smooth and starts to thicken. Add beaten egg yolks slowly and continue to cook and stir until mixture has thickened. Stir in ½ teaspoon vanilla. Put plums in a 12-inch glass pie dish and spoon custard over top of plums. (Some of the custard may sink to the bottom.) Whip the egg whites in a small mixer bowl until peaks start to form. Slowly add 3 tablespoons sugar and 1 teaspoon vanilla, continuing to beat until stiff peaks form. Spoon meringue over top of the custard. Sprinkle chopped nuts over top of meringue and bake at 425° F. for about 15 minutes, or until the meringue is golden brown. Remove from oven, let cool at room temperature, and then refrigerate until ready to serve. Spoon into dessert dishes. Serves 8.

LION HOUSE

Rhubarb Whip

4 cups rhubarb, cut in
   1-inch pieces

½ cup sugar

¼ cup water

1 package (3 ounces) straw-
   berry gelatin

½ cup cold water

½ cup whipping cream,
   whipped

Fresh strawberries (optional)

IN A LARGE SAUCEPAN COMBINE rhubarb, sugar, and water and bring to boil. Cover and cook on low heat 8 to 10 minutes. Remove from heat. Add gelatin and stir until it dissolves (about 2 minutes). Stir in cold water. Chill until partially set. Whip until fluffy. Fold in whipped cream and pour into sherbet glasses. Chill. Garnish with fresh strawberries and additional whipped cream, if desired. Makes about eight ½-cup servings.

LION HOUSE

Creamy Pineapple Sherbet

¼ cup sugar

1 envelope unflavored gelatin

½ cup water

1 15-ounce can crushed pineapple in juice, undrained

⅔ cup sugar

2 tablespoons honey

1 teaspoon vanilla

2 cups nonfat buttermilk

In a small saucepan, stir together ¼ cup sugar and gelatin; add water. Cook and stir over low heat until sugar and gelatin are dissolved. Remove from heat and cool the mixture slightly.

In a blender or food processor, combine pineapple with juice, ⅔ cup sugar, honey, vanilla, and gelatin mixture. Cover and blend until smooth. Stir in buttermilk.

Freeze the mixture in a 4-quart ice cream freezer according to the manufacturer's directions. Makes 12 servings.

Lion House

Joseph Fielding Smith's Favorite Sherbet

5 cups sugar

1 teaspoon salt

3 tablespoons cornstarch

2 quarts water

1 quart whipping cream

2 quarts milk

Juice of 6 oranges

Juice of 2 lemons

1 16-ounce can crushed pineapple and juice

3 or 4 bananas, mashed

In a large saucepan combine sugar, salt, cornstarch, and water. Cook till clear, then cool. Add whipping cream and milk. Add orange juice and lemon juice, crushed pineapple, and mashed bananas. Pour into 8-quart ice cream freezer and freeze. (Cut recipe in half to make 4 quarts.)

Source: Amelia Smith McConkie, daughter of President Joseph Fielding Smith.

Lion House

Fresh Grapefruit Sorbet

½ cup cold water

1 teaspoon unflavored
gelatin powder

⅔ cup diced pink grapefruit
sections

1 cup pink grapefruit juice

⅓ cup sugar

1 tablespoon lemon juice

IN A LARGE SAUCEPAN, COMBINE cold water and gelatin. Cook and stir over low heat until gelatin is dissolved. Remove from heat and stir in diced grapefruit, grapefruit juice, sugar, and lemon juice. Pour into ice-cube trays or an 8-inch square baking pan, and freeze until almost firm.

Break frozen mixture into chunks and place in blender or food processor. Blend several seconds, until fluffy but not thawed. Return to freezer trays and freeze until firm. Makes 6 servings.

LION HOUSE

Strawberry-Banana Sorbet

1 medium ripe banana

3 cups frozen unsweetened
strawberries

½ cup frozen concentrated
cranberry-juice cocktail

1 tablespoon light corn
syrup

WRAP PEELED BANANA IN PLASTIC and freeze until solid (at least 2 hours). In a food processor or blender, puree the strawberries until very smooth. Add the juice concentrate and continue blending until smooth, about 1 minute. Slice the frozen banana and add slices a few at a time, continuing to blend until completely smooth. Blend in corn syrup. May be served immediately, or placed in a chilled bowl, covered, and frozen for 30 minutes. Sorbet will keep in freezer for up to 1 week; let soften slightly before serving. Makes 6 servings.

LION HOUSE

Melon Sorbet

1 cup orange juice

¼ cup sugar

2 cups chopped cantaloupe,
   honeydew, or water-
   melon

½ cup light cream

3 tablespoons lemon juice

Food coloring, if desired

2 egg whites

¼ cup sugar

Bring orange juice and ¼ cup sugar to boil in a small saucepan over medium-high heat, stirring occasionally. Reduce heat to low; simmer for 5 minutes. Cool. Blend melon and light cream in a blender or food processor until smooth, about 1 minute. Stir in the lemon juice and cooled orange juice mixture. If using honeydew, you may wish to add a few drops of green food coloring; for watermelon, use red food coloring. Pour mixture into a 9-inch square baking pan; cover and freeze until firm, about 4 hours. Chill a mixer bowl during this time for later use.

Using an electric mixer, beat egg whites until soft peaks form. Gradually add ¼ cup sugar, beating until stiff peaks form.

Place frozen mixture in chilled mixer bowl. Break into chunks and beat with electric mixer until fluffy but not melted. Fold in beaten egg whites. Return to baking pan. Cover and freeze for several hours or until firm. Remove from freezer about 5 minutes before serving to soften slightly. Makes 6 servings.

Lion House

Snowballs

Vanilla ice cream

Toasted coconut or chopped
   pecans

Chocolate, caramel, or
   other favorite topping

Maraschino cherries

Scoop ice cream with large ice cream scoop into desired size balls. Make balls as rounded and smooth as possible. Drop ice cream balls into bowl of chopped pecans or toasted coconut and roll around until well coated. Place on cookie sheet that has been lined with wax paper or plastic wrap. Make an indentation on the top of each snowball with your thumb. Place pan in freezer until time to serve. At serving time, place snowballs in individual serving bowls. Pour a small amount of chocolate, caramel, or other favorite topping on top of snowball and top with a stemmed maraschino cherry.

To toast coconut: Spread desired amount of coconut on a cookie sheet and put in the oven at 350° F. for 3 to 5 minutes or until light golden brown. Coconut will continue to brown a little after you remove it from the oven.

Note: Snowballs can be made up to one week ahead, if they are well covered after they are frozen solid.

Lion House

Harvest Peach Ice Cream

8 large fresh peaches

Juice of 2 lemons

3 cups sugar

1 14-ounce can sweetened
    condensed milk

2 cups whipping cream,
    whipped

1 quart milk

PEEL PEACHES; MASH IN A LARGE BOWL. Mix with lemon juice and sugar and let stand in refrigerator for two hours. Mix peach mixture with sweetened condensed milk, whipped cream, and milk. Pour into 4-quart ice cream freezer can. Freeze according to freezer directions. Makes 4 quarts.

LION HOUSE

Frosty Vanilla Ice Cream

4 junket tablets

¼ cup cold water

2 quarts milk

2 cups whipping cream

2 cups sugar

⅛ teaspoon salt

4 teaspoons vanilla

IN A SMALL BOWL DISSOLVE JUNKET tablets in cold water. In a large saucepan mix milk, cream, sugar, and salt, and heat to lukewarm. Add dissolved junket tablets and vanilla. Pour into freezer can. Put dasher in place and let stand 10 minutes to set. Then freeze according to freezer directions. Makes 4 quarts.

Variations: Add 2 cups mashed fresh or frozen fruit (thawed), such as raspberries, strawberries, peaches, or boysenberries.

LION HOUSE

VERY BERRY PIE.
RECIPE ON PAGE 70.

Pie Tips

BRUSH THE EDGES OF PIE CRUSTS WITH WATER JUST before putting the top crust on. This will help seal them together.

For a beautiful golden top, brush pie crust with cream, half-and-half, evaporated milk, or regular milk and sprinkle with sugar before baking.

Make 4 to 8 pies at a time, bake them, and freeze them in gallon Ziplock® bags. Once pies are frozen they can be stacked on top of each other. When you have company, take a frozen pie out of the plastic bag and bake at 325° F. for 35 to 40 minutes. You'll have a nice warm pie and no mess in the kitchen.

Keep pie shells from shrinking by always pricking holes in them before baking. Then do one of the following: bake shells on the bottom of an upside-down pie tin; or, after lining pie tin with dough, line it with aluminum foil and then pour beans, wheat, or rice in it and bake for half the baking time. Lift out the foil and its contents and continue baking the shell for the remainder of the baking time.

LION HOUSE

Method for Assembling All Fruit Pies

SPOON PIE FILLING INTO AN UNBAKED 9-inch pie shell. Brush the flat edge of the dough with water and place the top crust on pie. Seal the 2 crusts together by gently pressing around the flat edge of the pie tin. Cut the excess dough off from around the edge. Brush milk (or cream, half-and-half, or evaporated milk) on the top of the pie, being careful not to get it too close to the edge of the pie. Sprinkle sugar on top of the milk and bake at 375° F. for 45 to 50 minutes or until golden brown. If the pie crust cracks open or filling comes out the sides, the pie is overdone.

LION HOUSE

Lion House Pie Dough

¼ cup butter

⅓ cup lard

¼ cup margarine

⅓ cup shortening

1 tablespoon sugar

½ teaspoon baking powder

1 teaspoon salt

1 tablespoon nonfat dry milk
   (powdered)

1½ cups pastry flour*

1½ cups bread flour*

½ cup cold water (may need
   1 tablespoon more
   water)

IN A MIXER, CREAM TOGETHER BUTTER, lard, margarine, and shortening. In a bowl, mix the sugar, baking powder, salt, and dry milk powder together. Then add to the creamed butter mixture and mix briefly. Add pastry flour and beat until it is blended. Add bread flour and mix slightly. Pour water in and beat again only until water is incorporated.

Divide dough into two or three balls. Roll out on floured board. Line pie pan with dough and cut off excess dough. For baked pie shells, flute edges. Prick holes in bottom with fork and bake at 425° F. for 12 to 15 minutes or until light golden brown. For fruit pies and other pies that bake in the crust, fill pie shell and follow instructions for particular pie recipe you are using. Yields 2 to 3 pie shells.

All-purpose flour can be used instead of the combination of bread and pastry flour.

Note: This crust can also be made using the traditional pie crust method: by hand-cutting fats into the dry ingredients.

LION HOUSE

Lite Pie Crust

⅓ cup margarine, cut in
   small pieces

1 cup flour

⅓ cup ice water

1 egg white

1½ teaspoons white vinegar

¼ teaspoon salt

IN A SMALL BOWL, CUT MARGARINE into flour with a fork until mixture resembles coarse meal. Combine water, egg white, vinegar, and salt in a small bowl; mix well. Add liquid mixture to flour mixture. Mix lightly with a fork until mixture forms a ball. Refrigerate for at least ½ hour before rolling out dough. Makes one 9-inch pie shell, or pastry for a 1-crust pie.

For baked pie shell: Roll pastry in a circle; fit into pie tin. Flute edges. Prick in several places with fork. Bake at 425° F. for 12 to 15 minutes or until light golden brown.

LION HOUSE

Apple Pie

Pastry for 2-crust pie
4 to 5 cups tart apples,
    peeled, cored, and
    sliced*
¼ to ½ cup water
¾ to 1 cup sugar
1 to 2 tablespoons flour
½ to 1 teaspoon cinnamon
⅛ teaspoon salt
1 tablespoon lemon juice
2 tablespoons butter or
    margarine

PUT APPLES IN A LARGE SAUCEPAN and steam or gently simmer in water until they wilt and begin to become transparent. (This is a partial cooking only so that apples will cook thoroughly in the pie.)

Combine sugar, flour, cinnamon, and salt in a small bowl. Mix well. Spread half of mixture over the pastry-lined pie pan. Lift apples from cooking liquid into crust. Add ¼ cup of the cooking liquid. Sprinkle with remaining sugar mixture. Sprinkle pie filling with lemon juice and dot with butter. Roll, fit, and seal top crust. Brush with milk and sprinkle with sugar, if desired.

Bake on lower shelf of oven at 425° F. for 30 to 40 minutes, or until nicely browned.

Note: Apple pie is only as good as the apples it is made with. Tart, juicy apples are desirable, and some judgment is necessary as to amounts of sugar and thickening when sweeter, less juicy apples are used.

LION HOUSE

Swiss Apple-Cherry Pie

Pastry for 2-crust pie
4 tart apples
6 tablespoons butter or
    margarine
1 cup sugar
2 tablespoons flour
2 teaspoons cinnamon
½ teaspoon nutmeg
1 21-ounce can pitted sour
    red cherries, drained
½ teaspoon sugar
¼ teaspoon cinnamon

PARE, CORE, AND SLICE APPLES. Melt 2 tablespoons butter and brush on bottom of pastry shell. Arrange a layer of sliced apples on bottom of shell. In a bowl, mix together sugar, flour, cinnamon, and nutmeg; then sprinkle about ¼ of this mixture over layer of apples. Arrange layer of cherries and sprinkle with ¼ of the sugar mixture. Repeat this step three more times, alternating with layers of apples and cherries, and ending with apples. Cover each layer of fruit with ¼ of sugar mixture, except last layer.

Dot top of last layer with remaining 4 tablespoons of butter. In a bowl, mix together ½ teaspoon sugar and ¼ teaspoon cinnamon. Place top crust on pie, then brush with cream or evaporated milk and sprinkle with cinnamon and sugar mixture. Cut vents in top crust. Bake at 425° F. for 30 to 40 minutes. Serve warm with a scoop of vanilla ice cream.

LION HOUSE

Cherry Pie

Pastry for 2-crust pie
2½ tablespoons quick-
    cooking tapioca
⅛ teaspoon salt
1 cup sugar
6 drops red food coloring
3 cups drained water-packed
    red sour cherries
½ cup cherry juice
¼ teaspoon almond extract
1 tablespoon butter

IN A LARGE BOWL COMBINE ALL ingredients except pastry and butter. Let stand about 15 minutes. Pour into pie shell; dot filling with butter. Cut air vents in top crust and place over filling; press top and bottom crusts together on edge of pie pan. Crimp or flute. Bake pie at 375° F. for about 50 minutes.

LION HOUSE

Raisin Apple Pie

Pastry for 2-crust pie
¾ cup raisins
1½ cups water
½ cup sugar
1 tablespoon lemon juice
¼ teaspoon salt
2 tablespoons butter
¾ teaspoon vanilla
2 tablespoons cornstarch
2 tablespoons water
1½ cups sliced apples
    (water-packed canned,
    drained)
¼ cup walnuts, coarsely
    chopped

IN A LARGE SAUCEPAN, BOIL RAISINS and 1½ cups water together for 15 minutes. Add sugar, lemon juice, salt, butter, and vanilla. Cook until the butter is melted. In a small bowl, mix together cornstarch and 2 tablespoons water, then slowly add to the raisin mixture, stirring continuously.

Cook until thick. Mix apples and walnuts together in a separate bowl. Add to the raisin mixture. Mix together and fill pies. Bake at 375° F. for about 50 minutes. Yields 1 double-crust pie.

LION HOUSE

Raisin Pie

Pastry for 2-crust pie
1½ cups raisins
2 cups water
¼ cup pineapple juice
¼ cup lemon juice
1 cup sugar
¾ teaspoon vanilla
¼ cup cornstarch
¼ teaspoon salt

PREHEAT OVEN TO 375° F. IN A small saucepan combine raisins, water, pineapple juice, lemon juice, ½ cup sugar, and vanilla. Bring to a boil and cook 5 minutes. Pour mixture through strainer. Reserve liquid in pan and set raisins aside.

Mix together ½ cup sugar, cornstarch, and salt; add to hot raisin liquid and beat together with a wire whisk. Continue cooking and stirring until thick, about 5 minutes. Add raisins back into liquid and pour into unbaked pie shell.

Roll out top crust. Cut two 2-inch slits near center, then snip with scissors at sides and between slits, or make any fancy cutout design desired. (This will allow steam to escape during baking.) Place top crust on center of pie. Pull slits slightly apart, if necessary, with a knife. Seal crusts together and flute edges. Bake for about 45 to 50 minutes or to the desired browness. Makes 1 double-crust pie.

LION HOUSE

Pineapple Pie

Pastry for 2-crust pie
2 20-ounce cans pineapple
    tidbits in juice
1 cup sugar
3 tablespoons cornstarch
¼ teaspoon salt
1 drop yellow food coloring

PREHEAT OVEN TO 375° F. POUR pineapple in a bowl. Discard ¾ cup of the juice; keep the rest. Mix sugar, cornstarch, and salt together in a bowl; pour on top of pineapple. Mix well with a rubber spatula. Add food coloring and mix well. Fill crust, add top crust, and bake for 45 to 50 minutes or until golden brown. Makes 1 pie.

LION HOUSE

Apricot Pineapple Pie

Pastry for 2-crust pie

15¼-ounce can apricot
    halves

20-ounce can pineapple
    tidbits

¾ cup sugar

¼ cup plus 2 tablespoons
    cornstarch

¼ teaspoon salt

PREHEAT OVEN TO 375° F. Discard ¼ cup of apricot juice. Pour apricots and remaining juice in a large mixing bowl. Cut apricots in half, so each piece is ¼ of an apricot. Discard ½ cup of pineapple juice. Add pineapple tidbits and remaining juice to apricots. In a separate bowl, mix together sugar, cornstarch, and salt; pour on top of fruit. Mix well with a rubber spatula. Fill crust, add top crust, and bake at 375° F. for 45 to 50 minutes or until golden brown. Makes 1 pie.

LION HOUSE

Peach Pie

Pastry for 2-crust pie

1 29-ounce can peach slices

½ cup sugar

¼ cup plus 2 tablespoons
    instant starch

¼ teaspoon salt

⅛ teaspoon cinnamon

PREHEAT OVEN TO 375° F. Discard ½ cup juice from peaches. Pour peaches and remaining juice into a large mixing bowl. In a separate bowl, mix together sugar, cornstarch, salt, and cinnamon; pour on top of peaches. Mix well with a rubber spatula. Fill crust, add top crust, and bake for 45 to 50 minutes or until golden brown. Makes 1 pie.

LION HOUSE

Boysenberry Pie

Pastry for 2-crust pie
1 16-ounce bag frozen
    boysenberries, thawed
1 cup sugar
¼ teaspoon salt
2½ tablespoons cornstarch

PREHEAT OVEN TO 375° F. POUR thawed berries and juice in a large mixing bowl. In a separate bowl, mix together sugar, salt, and cornstarch; pour on top of berries. Mix well with a rubber spatula. Fill crust, add top crust, and bake for 45 to 50 minutes or until golden brown. Makes 1 pie.

LION HOUSE

Blueberry Pie

Pastry for 2-crust pie
1 16-ounce bag frozen
    blueberries, thawed
1 cup sugar
¼ teaspoon salt
4 tablespoons cornstarch

PREHEAT OVEN TO 375° F. POUR thawed berries and juice in a large mixing bowl. In a separate bowl, mix together sugar, salt, and cornstarch; pour on top of berries. Mix well with a rubber spatula. Fill crust, add top crust, and bake for 45 to 50 minutes or until golden brown. Makes 1 pie.

LION HOUSE

Very Berry Pie

Pastry for two 2-crust pies

1 16-ounce bag frozen
   boysenberries (no sugar
   added)

1 8-ounce bag frozen blueberries (no sugar added)

1 8-ounce bag frozen
   raspberries (no sugar
   added)

1¾ cups sugar

½ teaspoon salt

½ cup cornstarch

PREHEAT OVEN TO 375° F. THAW ALL berries, then pour berries and all of the juice in a mixing bowl. In a separate bowl, mix together sugar, salt, and cornstarch; pour on top of berries. Mix well with a rubber spatula. Fill crusts, add top crusts, and bake for 45 to 50 minutes or until golden brown. Makes 2 pies.

Pictured on page 60.

LION HOUSE

Fresh Strawberry Pie

1 Lite Pie Crust baked pie
   shell

3 cups water

1 cup sugar

1 3-ounce package
   strawberry-flavored
   gelatin

3 tablespoons cornstarch

3 cups fresh strawberries,
   washed and hulled

IN A MEDIUM SAUCEPAN, BRING water and sugar to a boil. Mix gelatin with cornstarch; gradually add to boiling mixture. Cook over medium-high heat, stirring constantly, for 5 minutes or until mixture is clear and thickened slightly. Let stand at room temperature until just warm, about 15 minutes. While mixture is cooling wash and hull strawberries; put them in a large mixing bowl. Pour gelatin mixture over fresh strawberries and fold together gently. Mound in baked pie shell. Chill for at least 1 hour before serving. Top with low-fat whipped topping, if desired. Makes 8 servings.

LION HOUSE

Rhubarb Pie

Pastry for 2-crust pie
4 cups rhubarb (frozen,
    partially thawed)*
1¾ cups sugar
¼ cup all-purpose flour
2 tablespoons cornstarch
¼ teaspoon salt
1 egg
1 drop red food coloring

PREHEAT OVEN TO 400° F. PLACE rhubarb in a medium mixing bowl and let thaw for 10 to 15 minutes. Drain liquid. In a separate bowl, combine sugar, flour, cornstarch, and salt. Beat egg, then blend with the flour mixture. Add rhubarb and red food coloring. Mix well. Pour into unbaked 9-inch pie shell. Roll out top crust; cut slits and place over filling. Seal, then flute edges. Brush top with milk and sprinkle with sugar, if desired. Bake for 45 minutes or until nicely browned. Makes 1 double-crust pie.

Make fresh rhubarb pie by substituting 4 cups fresh rhubarb. Follow the recipe and directions, except bake at 350° F. for 50 to 55 minutes.

LION HOUSE

Cranberry Pie

Baked 9-inch pie shell
2½ cups raw cranberries
1 cup water
1 cup sugar
4 tablespoons cornstarch
½ cup raisins
½ cup chopped walnuts
2 tablespoons butter
1 cup whipping cream,
    whipped

IN MEDIUM SAUCEPAN COOK cranberries in water until skins pop. Strain and save juice in pan. Mix sugar and cornstarch together, then add slowly to juice. Cook until thickened, stirring constantly. Stir in raisins, nuts, cooked cranberries, and butter. Pour into baked pie shell. Chill.

When ready to serve, garnish with whipped cream. Makes 1 pie.

LION HOUSE

Two-Crust Cranberry Pie

Pastry for 2-crust pie
2 cups raw cranberries
1 cup water
1 cup sugar
1¾ tablespoons cornstarch
¼ to ½ cup chopped walnuts
2 teaspoons butter or
    margarine

In medium saucepan cook cranberries in water until skins pop. Strain and save the juice in pan. Mix sugar and cornstarch together, then add to juice. Cook mixture until it thickens and bubbles, stirring constantly. Stir in walnuts, cranberries, and butter.

Pour into pie shell, add top crust, and bake at 400° F. for 10 minutes. Reduce heat to 350° F. and bake for 45 minutes more or until crust is nicely browned. Makes 1 pie.

Lion House

Eclairs

1 cup cold water
½ cup butter or margarine
1 cup all-purpose flour
¼ teaspoon salt
4 eggs, fresh, at room
    temperature
Vanilla pudding

Preheat oven to 375° F. In a large saucepan, bring water and margarine to a rolling boil. While the water and margarine are boiling and still on the stove, add flour and salt. Stir until the mixture clings together. Remove from stove and place in a medium mixer. Add one egg at a time, mixing on low speed until each egg is incorporated. The batter should be shiny and smooth. Do not overwhip; too much air causes the shells to be bumpy and misshapen. Force dough through a decorating tube onto paper-lined baking sheets in strips about 3 inches long. Bake at 375° F. for 25 minutes.

When pastry is cool, slice off tops and scoop out any uncooked dough that may be remaining. Fill with vanilla pudding. Replace tops. Frost with Chocolate Ganache (see recipe on page 118) or Chocolate Frosting. Chill until ready to serve.

Chocolate Frosting
4 tablespoons cocoa
3 cups powdered sugar
4 tablespoons butter or
    margarine, softened
2 or 3 tablespoons milk
1 teaspoon vanilla

Mix cocoa and powdered sugar in mixing bowl. Add butter, milk, and vanilla. Beat until smooth. Makes approximately 36 eclairs.

Lion House

Puff Pastry

1 cup flour
¼ teaspoon salt
½ cup butter (or ¼ cup
    shortening and ¼ cup
    butter)
1 cup boiling water
4 eggs

SIFT FLOUR WITH SALT. COMBINE butter (or butter and shortening) with boiling water in saucepan; keep on low heat until butter is melted. Add flour all at once, stirring vigorously until mixture forms a ball and leaves sides of pan. Cook about 2 minutes until mixture is very dry. Remove from heat.

Add unbeaten eggs one at a time and beat well after each addition. Continue beating until mixture forms a thick dough. To make cream puffs, cocktail puffs, or puff shells follow directions below.

TO MAKE CREAM PUFFS: Preheat oven to 425° F. Drop dough by tablespoonfuls, about 2 inches apart, onto baking sheet lined with wax paper. Bake about 10 to 15 minutes. Reduce heat to 400° F. and bake 5 to 10 minutes, then reduce heat to 375° F. for another 5 to 10 minutes. Bake about 30 to 40 minutes total, or until beads of moisture no longer appear on the surface. Do not open oven door during early part of baking. Remove from oven and place on wire racks to cool.

When cool, cut a slit in side of each puff; remove doughy centers if necessary. Fill with a cream filling made from a pudding and pie filling mix, following package directions, or fill with sweetened whipped cream, or with any other favorite cream filling. Makes about 12 large cream puff shells.

TO MAKE COCKTAIL PUFFS: Follow directions for baking cream puffs, except drop by small teaspoonfuls onto baking sheet lined with wax paper. Bake for a total of about 20 to 30 minutes. Fill with any savory filling. Makes 4 to 5 dozen small puffs.

TO MAKE PUFF SHELLS: Drop dough by tablespoonfuls into deep hot fat (375° F.). Fry 10 to 15 minutes, turning often, or until a good crust forms. Drain well, then cut top off each shell. Fill hot shells with creamed fish, poultry, meat, eggs, or vegetables. Or cool the shells and fill with a salad mixture, such as chicken salad. Replace tops before serving. Makes about 12 large shells.

LION HOUSE AND JOSEPH SMITH BUILDING

Chocolate Party Puffs

Cocktail puffs (make 60
    puffs)
1 quart vanilla ice cream
1 quart heavy cream,
    whipped
1 tablespoon sugar, or to
    taste
1 teaspoon vanilla, or to
    taste
1 cup chocolate syrup
1 16-ounce jar maraschino
    cherries, well drained

MAKE COCKTAIL PUFFS ACCORDING to directions. (Recipe on page 73.) Slit cooled puffs and pull out any dough strands that may be inside. Fill shells with vanilla ice cream. Freeze on a tray in a single layer. When frozen pack in plastic bags and store in freezer until ready to use.

To assemble, whip the cream; add sugar, vanilla, and chocolate syrup. Fold slightly thawed puffs and cherries into the cream. Serve immediately from a glass bowl. Makes 20 servings of 3 puffs each.

LION HOUSE

Lemon Cream Pie

Baked 9-inch pie shell
1¼ cups sugar
¼ teaspoon salt
6 tablespoons cornstarch
1½ cups boiling water
3 eggs, slightly beaten
6 tablespoons lemon juice
¼ teaspoon grated lemon
    rind
2 tablespoons butter or
    margarine
1 cup heavy cream, whipped
    and sweetened

COMBINE SUGAR, SALT, AND cornstarch in a 2- or 3-quart saucepan. Blend well. Place over medium heat and add boiling water, stirring rapidly until smooth and thick. Bring to a full boil to thoroughly cook the cornstarch. Remove from heat. In a medium bowl slightly beat eggs. Add a little of the hot pudding to the eggs while stirring rapidly. Return egg mixture to hot pudding in saucepan and reheat, stirring constantly, just until smooth. Remove from heat and add lemon juice and rind and butter. Pour into baked pie shell. Cover surface with plastic wrap to prevent a skin from forming. Chill. Served topped with whipped cream.

LION HOUSE

Ezra Taft Benson's Lemon Meringue Pie

Baked 9-inch pie shell

Grated rind from 2 lemons

3 cups sugar

2 heaping tablespoons flour

2 heaping tablespoons cornstarch

5 egg yolks, well beaten

4 cups water

Juice of 2 lemons

1 tablespoon butter

5 egg whites

3 tablespoons sugar

IN A LARGE SAUCEPAN GRATE outside rind of 2 lemons; add sugar, flour, and cornstarch. Stir in beaten egg yolks, then water and lemon juice. Cook over medium heat, stirring constantly till the mixture is thickened. Stir in butter. Pour into baked pie shell.

To make meringue, beat egg whites until foamy; stir in 3 tablespoons sugar and continue beating until stiff. Carefully spoon onto pie. Bake at 425° to 450° F. for 3 to 5 minutes, or till meringue is lightly browned.

Source: Flora Amussen Benson, wife of President Ezra Taft Benson.

LION HOUSE

Lemon Pie

Baked 9-inch pie shell

1½ cups sugar

7 tablespoons cornstarch

5 egg yolks

2 cups water

½ cup lemon juice

2 tablespoons butter

IN A BOWL, MIX TOGETHER SUGAR and cornstarch; pour mixture in top of a double boiler* not yet on the pan of water.

Place 5 eggs yolks in a bowl and whisk until well mixed. Slowly pour ⅛ cup of water into egg yolks while whisking. Pour in remaining water, then pour egg mixture into the double boiler with the sugar mixture. Add lemon juice; stir well.

Place double boiler on top of water pan and cook, stirring well every 6 to 7 minutes for 30 to 40 minutes or until thick and clear. (It is very important to stir often or the cornstarch will make large lumps.) Remove from heat. Cut butter into pieces and add to hot mixture. Stir until butter is dissolved and well blended. Pour into baked pie shell. Top with meringue or whipped cream. (For instructions on making meringue, see recipe for Ezra Taft Benson's Lemon Meringue Pie on this page.) Makes 1 pie.

Pudding can be made in a stainless steel bowl that fits on a pan of water if a double boiler is not available.

LION HOUSE

Lemon Truffle Pie

Baked 9-inch pie shell
½ cup water
2 tablespoons sugar
1 egg
1 tablespoon cornstarch
1 tablespoon sugar
1½ tablespoons fresh lemon
    juice
Zest of ½ lemon
1½ teaspoons butter
1 cup vanilla chips
1 8-ounce package cream
    cheese
½ cup whipped cream,
    sweetened
1 tablespoon toasted
    almonds

Put water and 2 tablespoons sugar in saucepan and bring to a boil. In a large bowl, mix egg, cornstarch, 1 tablespoon sugar, and lemon juice. Slowly add hot water to egg mixture in bowl; then pour entire mixture back into pan. Heat until thickened, stirring often. Remove from heat and add zest of lemon and butter. Stir until mixed and cool.

Pour two-thirds of filling in bowl. Add vanilla chips to the filling remaining in pan. Stir until chips are melted. Place cream cheese in bowl. Add filling with vanilla chips to cream cheese and beat together. Spread this mixture in bottom of pie shell. Spread remaining two-thirds of lemon filling on top. Chill for two hours.

Top with whipped cream and garnish with toasted almonds or sprinkle toasted almonds over whipped cream and serve on side. Makes 1 pie.

Pictured on page 77.

Carriage Court

Key Lime Pie

1½ cups graham cracker
    crumbs
6 tablespoons melted butter
    or margarine
1½ cups sugar
7 tablespoons cornstarch
3 egg yolks
2 cups water
½ cup lime juice
2 tablespoons butter (cut
    into pieces)
1 drop green food coloring

In a 9-inch pie pan, mix graham cracker crumbs with melted butter. Use a fork and level well, then press firmly into bottom and sides of pan.

Mix together sugar and cornstarch and place in top of a double boiler not yet on the pan of water.

Place egg yolks in a bowl and whisk until well mixed. Slowly pour half of the water into egg yolks while whisking together. Pour in remaining water. Add egg mixture to sugar mixture. Add lime juice and mix well.

Place on top of double boiler with water in it. Turn heat on high and cook, stirring every 6 to 7 minutes for 30 to 40 minutes until mixture is clear and thick. (It is important to stir often or the cornstarch will make large lumps.) Cut butter into pieces and add to filling. Add food coloring and stir until well blended. Pour into graham cracker crust. Chill. Makes 1 pie.

Lion House

LEMON TRUFFLE PIE.
RECIPE ON PAGE 76.

Pecan Pie

Pastry for 1-crust pie*
3 eggs, slightly beaten
2 cups plus 3 tablespoons
   sugar
½ teaspoon salt
½ cup plus 1½ tablespoons
   dark corn syrup
½ teaspoon vanilla
1½ tablespoons butter,
   melted
1½ cup pecans

IN A LARGE BOWL SLIGHTLY BEAT EGGS, then add sugar and whisk together with a wire whisk. Add salt, corn syrup, vanilla, and butter. Mix well.

Place pecans in bottom of an unbaked 9-inch pie shell. Pour filling evenly on top of pecans and bake at 350° F. for 50 to 60 minutes or until the filling is set. Allow to cool completely before cutting.

For easiest cutting, refrigerate until pie is completely cold. Carefully turn pie upside down and lay it on the counter. Remove pie tin. Use a knife that is as long as the pie is wide. Press the knife straight down through the pie to make the desired sizes. Carefully lift each piece of pie up, turn it over, and place on a plate. Makes 1 pie.

*Be sure to bake in 9-inch pie shell; an 8-inch shell will overflow.

LION HOUSE

Pumpkin Pie

Pastry for 1-crust pie
1½ cups pumpkin
½ teaspoon cinnamon
½ teaspoon nutmeg
¼ teaspoon ginger
¼ teaspoon allspice
½ cup granulated sugar
⅓ cup brown sugar
1 teaspoon salt
1½ tablespoons cornstarch
2 eggs
1 cup evaporated milk
1 cup water
Whipped cream, if desired

PUT PUMPKIN IN A LARGE MIXING bowl. In a separate bowl, mix together cinnamon, nutmeg, ginger, allspice, granulated sugar, brown sugar, salt, and cornstarch. Add to the pumpkin and mix until blended. Add eggs and evaporated milk and mix until incorporated. Add water and mix well. Pour into an unbaked pie shell and bake at 375° F. for 50 to 60 minutes or until a knife inserted in the center comes out clean. Top with whipped cream, if desired. Makes 1 pie.

LION HOUSE

Rich Pumpkin Pie

Pastry for 1-crust pie

14 ounces pumpkin puree

2 tablespoons flour

½ teaspoon cinnamon

Pinch nutmeg

Pinch ginger

Pinch cloves

½ teaspoon salt

½ cup brown sugar

2 eggs

2 tablespoons corn syrup

1 cup milk

½ cup evaporated milk

PUT PUMPKIN, FLOUR, CINNAMON, nutmeg, ginger, cloves, salt, and brown sugar in a large bowl. Blend together. Slowly add eggs, corn syrup, milk, and evaporated milk. Mix well.

Pour into an unbaked 9-inch pie shell. Let sit 60 minutes and then bake at 375° F. for approximately 60 minutes or until a knife inserted in the center comes out clean. Makes 1 pie.

CARRIAGE COURT

Joseph F. Smith's Custard Pie

Pastry for 1-crust pie

2 cups milk

4 eggs

½ cup sugar

Pinch salt

Generous sprinkling nutmeg

PREHEAT OVEN TO 375° F. Put milk in a medium bowl. Beat eggs and strain through fine sieve into bowl of milk. Add sugar, salt, and nutmeg. Stir well and pour into pie shell. Bake until knife inserted in the center just barely comes out clean, about 50 to 60 minutes. Do not overcook, or custard will become watery. Makes 6 to 8 servings.

Note: This recipe does not call for vanilla.

Source: Salt Lake City 18th Ward Cookbook.

LION HOUSE

Chocolate Chip Pie

Chocolate pie shell
2 cups walnuts, chopped
4 eggs
6 tablespoons plus
    1 teaspoon sugar
1 cup brown sugar
2½ tablespoons corn syrup
1 cup flour
¾ pound semisweet
    chocolate chips
1½ cups butter

PREHEAT OVEN TO 350° F. CHOP walnuts and set aside. In a large mixing bowl, beat together eggs. Add sugar, brown sugar, and corn syrup. Add flour, chocolate chips, and chopped nuts.

Melt butter. Cool so it is still melted, but not too hot and add to mixture. Scoop into chocolate pie shell. Bake for 50 minutes. Makes 1 pie.

JOSEPH SMITH BUILDING

Baked Alaska Pie

1 8-inch baked pie shell
1 quart peppermint ice
    cream
2 to 3 tablespoons chocolate
    syrup (or ½ cup fudge
    ice cream topping and
    1 tablespoon evaporated
    milk)
5 egg whites
1 teaspoon vanilla
½ teaspoon cream of tartar
⅔ cup sugar

SPOON ICE CREAM INTO PIE SHELL. Drizzle with chocolate syrup.* Place in freezer until ready to use.

Heat oven to 500° F. Beat egg whites, vanilla, and cream of tartar until foamy. Gradually beat in sugar until mixture is stiff and glossy. Remove pie from freezer. Completely cover ice cream in pie shell with meringue, sealing well to edge of crust and piling high. (If desired, pie may be frozen up to 24 hours at this point.)

When ready to serve, bake pie on lowest oven rack for 3 to 5 minutes or until meringue is light brown. Serve immediately. (Or again return to freezer until ready to serve.) Makes 6 to 8 servings.

*Fudge sauce may be substituted for chocolate syrup. To make fudge sauce, combine ½ cup fudge ice cream topping with 1 tablespoon evaporated milk in small saucepan and stir over medium heat until well blended. Make a one-fourth inch indentation in entire top of ice cream, leaving a little ridge around the edge of pie. Evenly distribute fudge sauce in indentation.

LION HOUSE

Black Forest Pie

Pastry for 1-crust pie

Filling

¾ cup butter or margarine
¾ cup sugar
6 tablespoons unsweetened
  cocoa
⅔ cup ground blanched
  almonds
2 tablespoons flour
3 eggs, separated
2 tablespoons water
¼ cup sugar

PREHEAT OVEN TO 350° F. In a medium saucepan, melt butter or margarine; stir in ¾ cup sugar and cocoa. Remove from heat and allow to cool for 5 minutes. Add almonds and flour; stir well. Add egg yolks one at a time, stirring well after each addition. Stir in water. In a mixer bowl beat egg whites at high speed until foamy. Gradually add ¼ cup sugar, beating all the time, until soft peaks form. Fold chocolate mixture into egg whites just until blended. Pour mixture into unbaked pastry shell. Bake for 35 to 45 minutes or until wooden toothpick inserted in center comes out clean. Cool 5 minutes.

Topping

⅓ cup sour cream
2 tablespoons sugar
½ teaspoon vanilla
1 cup canned cherry pie
  filling

IN A MEDIUM BOWL, combine sour cream, sugar, and vanilla. Spread over warm pie. Spoon cherry pie filling over the top and return pie to oven for 5 minutes.

Glaze

½ cup semisweet chocolate
  chips
1½ teaspoons shortening

MELT CHOCOLATE CHIPS and shortening over low heat in a small saucepan, stirring constantly. Drizzle over pie and refrigerate for at least 2 hours. Serves 8.

LION HOUSE

Four-Step Black Bottom Pie

Crust

36 gingersnaps

½ cup butter or margarine, melted

Dash salt

Filling

4 cups milk

4 tablespoons butter or margarine

½ cup cornstarch

1½ cups sugar

4 egg yolks, slightly beaten

2 teaspoons vanilla

2 squares baking chocolate

2 envelopes (2 tablespoons) unflavored gelatin

½ cup cold water

4 egg whites, beaten stiff

1 cup sugar

1 teaspoon cream of tartar

2 teaspoons imitation rum flavoring

1 cup whipped cream, sweetened, if desired

CRUSH 36 GINGERSNAPS; ROLL fine and combine with ½ cup melted butter or margarine and a dash of salt. Mold evenly into an 11-inch springform pan. Set aside.

Step 1: In a large saucepan scald milk; add butter. Combine cornstarch and sugar in a small bowl; moisten with enough water to make paste. Stir paste into scalded milk and cook until mixture comes to a boil, stirring constantly. Stir hot mixture gradually into slightly beaten egg yolks. Return to heat and cook 2 minutes. Add vanilla. Remove 2 cups of custard. Add chocolate to the custard and beat well. Pour into the crumb crust and chill.

Step 2: Blend gelatin with cold water. Let it swell a few minutes, then fold into the remaining hot custard; let cool.

Step 3: Beat egg whites, 1 cup sugar, and cream of tartar into a meringue. Add rum flavoring and fold into custard from step 2.

Step 4: As soon as the chocolate custard has set, pour plain custard on top and chill until set. Serve with whipped cream and bits of chocolate for decoration.

LION HOUSE

Chocolate Cream Pie

2 baked 9-inch pie shells
1 quart milk
2 cups half-and-half
2 tablespoons butter
¾ cup sugar
3 egg yolks
½ cup sugar
¼ teaspoon salt
½ cup cornstarch
⅔ cup plus a few semisweet
    chocolate chips
1½ teaspoons vanilla
Whipped cream

RESERVE UP TO 1 CUP OF MILK TO mix with cornstarch. Place remaining milk in top of a double boiler and add half-and-half, butter, and ¾ cup sugar. Cook until butter is melted and milk looks scalded.

In a bowl, whisk egg yolks until well broken up; then add ½ cup sugar and salt and whisk together very well. Slowly add this mixture to the hot milk mixture, stirring constantly. Stir for approximately ½ minute and then allow to cook for 15 to 20 minutes. (This gives the eggs time to cook and start the thickening process. Undercooking at this point slows the finishing process down by as much as half an hour.)

Mix reserved milk and cornstarch together and slowly add to the hot mixture. Be careful to stir constantly or lumps will form. Continue to stir for at least 2 minutes and every 5 minutes for the next 15 to 20 minutes.

A good test to see if the pudding is done enough is to stand up the whisk in the middle of the pudding with the whisk touching the bottom of the pan. If the whisk will stay straight up after you let go, the pudding is thick enough.

When the pudding is thick enough, stir in chocolate chips. Stir well until chips are melted. Stir in vanilla. Remove the whole double boiler from stove (the hot water will help keep the pudding hot while you dish up the pies).

Pour filling into pie shells. Fill pies so the tops are a little rounded. When cool, top with whipped cream and garnish with chocolate chips, if desired. Makes 2 pies.

LION HOUSE

Coconut Cream Pie

2 baked 9-inch pie shells
1 quart milk
2 cups half-and-half
2 tablespoons butter
¾ cup sugar
3 egg yolks
½ cup sugar
¼ teaspoon salt
½ cup cornstarch
1½ teaspoons vanilla
1 cup coconut, loosely
    measured
Whipped cream
¼ cup coconut, toasted

RESERVE UP TO 1 CUP OF MILK to mix with cornstarch. Place remaining milk in top of a double boiler and add half-and-half, butter, and ¾ cup sugar. Cook until butter is melted and milk looks scalded.

In a bowl, whisk egg yolks until well broken up; then add ½ cup sugar and salt and whisk together very well. Slowly add this mixture to the hot milk mixture, stirring constantly. Stir for approximately ½ minute and then allow to cook for 15 to 20 minutes. (This gives the eggs time to cook and start the thickening process. Undercooking at this point slows the finishing process down by as much as half an hour.)

Mix reserved milk and cornstarch together and slowly add to the hot mixture. Be careful to stir constantly or lumps will form. Continue to stir for at least 2 minutes and every 5 minutes for the next 15 to 20 minutes.

A good test to see if the pudding is done enough is to stand up the whisk in the middle of the pudding with the whisk touching the bottom of the pan. If the whisk will stay straight up after you let go, the pudding is thick enough.

When the pudding is thick enough, stir in vanilla. Stir in coconut and remove the whole double boiler from stove (the hot water will help keep the pudding hot while you dish up the pies).

Pour filling into pie shells. Fill pies so the tops are a little rounded. When cool, top with whipped cream and garnish with toasted coconut, if desired. Makes 2 pies.

LION HOUSE

Vanilla Cream Pie

2 baked 9-inch pie shells
1 quart milk
2 cups half-and-half
2 tablespoons butter
¾ cup sugar
3 egg yolks
½ cup sugar
¼ teaspoon salt
½ cup cornstarch
1½ teaspoons vanilla
Whipped cream

RESERVE UP TO 1 CUP OF MILK TO mix with cornstarch. Place remaining milk in top of a double boiler and add half-and-half, butter, and ¾ cup sugar. Cook until butter is melted and milk looks scalded.

In a bowl, whisk egg yolks until well broken up; then add ½ cup sugar and salt and whisk together very well. Slowly add this mixture to the hot milk mixture, stirring constantly. Stir for approximately ½ minute and then allow to cook for 15 to 20 minutes. (This gives the eggs time to cook and start the thickening process. Undercooking at this point slows the finishing process down by as much as half an hour.)

Mix reserved milk and cornstarch together and slowly add to the hot mixture. Be careful to stir constantly or lumps will form. Continue to stir for at least 2 minutes and every 5 minutes for the next 15 to 20 minutes.

A good test to see if the pudding is done enough is to stand up the whisk in the middle of the pudding with the whisk touching the bottom of the pan. If the whisk will stay straight up after you let go, the pudding is thick enough.

When the pudding is thick enough, stir in vanilla. Remove the whole double boiler from stove (the hot water will help keep the pudding hot while you dish up the pies).

Pour filling into pie shells. Fill pies so the tops are a little rounded. When cool, top with whipped cream. Makes 2 pies.

Variations: Vanilla cream pie can be topped with canned lemon, blueberry, cherry, or raspberry pie filling and served with a dollop of whipped cream.

LION HOUSE

Banana Cream Pie

2 baked 9-inch pie shells
1 quart milk
2 cups half-and-half
2 tablespoons butter
¾ cup sugar
3 egg yolks
½ cup sugar
¼ teaspoon salt
½ cup cornstarch
1½ teaspoons vanilla
2 to 3 bananas
Whipped cream

Reserve up to 1 CUP OF MILK TO mix with cornstarch. Place remaining milk in top of a double boiler and add half-and-half, butter, and ¾ cup sugar. Cook until butter is melted and milk looks scalded.

In a bowl, whisk egg yolks until well broken up; then add ½ cup sugar and salt and whisk together very well. Slowly add this mixture to the hot milk mixture, stirring constantly. Stir for approximately ½ minute and then allow to cook for 15 to 20 minutes. (This gives the eggs time to cook and start the thickening process. Undercooking at this point slows the finishing process down by as much as half an hour.)

Mix reserved milk and cornstarch together and slowly add to the hot mixture. Be careful to stir constantly or lumps will form. Continue to stir for at least 2 minutes and every 5 minutes for the next 15 to 20 minutes.

A good test to see if the pudding is done enough is to stand up the whisk in the middle of the pudding with the whisk touching the bottom of the pan. If the whisk will stay straight up after you let go, the pudding is thick enough.

When the pudding is thick enough, stir in vanilla. Remove the whole double boiler from stove (the hot water will help keep the pudding hot while you dish up the pies).

Slice bananas in bottom of each pie shell. Pour filling on top of bananas. Fill pies so the tops are a little rounded. The pies need to cool 2 to 3 hours before cutting. When cool, top with whipped cream and garnish with additional banana slices, if desired. Makes 2 pies.

LION HOUSE

Razanna Cream Pie

2 baked 9-inch pie shells
1 quart milk
2 cups half-and-half
2 tablespoons butter
¾ cup sugar
3 egg yolks
½ cup sugar
¼ teaspoon salt
½ cup cornstarch
1½ teaspoons vanilla
2 to 3 bananas
Raspberry glaze*
Whipped cream

RESERVE UP TO 1 CUP OF MILK TO mix with cornstarch. Place remaining milk in top of a double boiler and add half-and-half, butter, and ¾ cup sugar. Cook until butter is melted and milk looks scalded.

In a bowl, whisk egg yolks until well broken up; then add ½ cup sugar and salt and whisk together very well. Slowly add this mixture to the hot milk mixture, stirring constantly. Stir for approximately ½ minute and then allow to cook for 15 to 20 minutes. (This gives the eggs time to cook and start the thickening process. Undercooking at this point slows the finishing process down by as much as half an hour.)

Mix reserved milk and cornstarch together and slowly add to the hot mixture. Be careful to stir constantly or lumps will form. Continue to stir for at least 2 minutes and every 5 minutes for the next 15 to 20 minutes.

A good test to see if the pudding is done enough is to stand up the whisk in the middle of the pudding with the whisk touching the bottom of the pan. If the whisk will stay straight up after you let go, the pudding is thick enough.

When the pudding is thick enough, stir in vanilla. Remove the whole double boiler from stove (the hot water will help keep the pudding hot while you dish up the pies).

Slice bananas in bottom of each pie shell. Pour filling on top of bananas, leaving room for raspberry glaze. Spread raspberry glaze on top of cream filling and serve. Makes 2 pies.

*For raspberry glaze use canned raspberry pie filling or fresh or frozen raspberries.

LION HOUSE

Pineapple Cream Pie

Crust

¾ cup butter

1½ cups flour

½ cup chopped nuts

Pineapple Filling

1 20-ounce can crushed
pineapple in juice

⅓ cup cornstarch

4 egg yolks

1 tablespoon water

1 cup sugar

¼ teaspoon salt

2 cups whole milk

2 tablespoons butter or
margarine

1 teaspoon vanilla

Cream Cheese Filling

1 8-ounce package cream
cheese, softened

½ cup powdered sugar

½ teaspoon vanilla

⅓ cup finely chopped
macadamia nuts

⅓ cup reserved pineapple,
drained

Topping

1 cup whipping cream

¼ cup powdered sugar

Remaining pineapple, liquid
squeezed out

Chopped macadamia nuts

To make crust: Preheat oven to 375° F. In a medium bowl, mix together butter, flour, and nuts. Press into a 13x9x2-inch pan. Bake for 15 minutes or until golden brown. Cool completely.

To make pineapple filling: Measure 1 cup pineapple and juice, reserving remaining pineapple for cream cheese filling and topping. Drain juice from measured pineapple. Combine cornstarch, egg yolks, and water in a small bowl. Combine sugar, salt, milk, and drained pineapple in saucepan. Cook over medium heat, stirring constantly, until mixture comes almost to a boil. Reduce heat to low. Add egg yolk mixture slowly, stirring constantly; continue to cook and stir until thickened. Add butter or margarine and vanilla. Remove from heat, cover with wax paper, and refrigerate for 30 minutes, stirring once or twice.

To make cream cheese filling: Combine cream cheese and powdered sugar in a medium bowl. Beat with a fork until blended and smooth. Add vanilla, nuts, and drained pineapple. Mix well. Spread over cooled crust. Cover with Pineapple Filling.

To make topping: In a small bowl whip cream with powdered sugar until soft peaks form. Spread over pie and garnish with pineapple and nuts. (Make sure pineapple is well drained before placing on top of whipped cream.) Serve or refrigerate until ready to serve. Serves 15.

Lion House

Raisin Cream Pie

Pastry for 2-crust pie
1 cup seedless raisins
1½ cups water
¾ cup sugar
3 tablespoons cornstarch
¼ teaspoon salt
1 teaspoon vanilla
1 tablespoon butter
1 cup light cream

SPREAD RAISINS ON SHEET PAN TO DRY. Either dry for two days on counter or put in oven on 350° F. for 10 minutes. (Fresh raisins have an enzyme that will not allow cornstarch to work.) After raisins are dry, rinse and drain them. Then put them in a saucepan, add water, and boil slowly for 10 minutes.

In a bowl, mix together sugar, cornstarch, and salt. Add to raisin mixture and cook, stirring constantly, until clear and thick. Remove from heat and stir in vanilla and butter. Stir until butter is melted and mixture is slightly cool. Stir in cream and allow filling to cool completely. Pour filling into unbaked pie shell and cover with top crust. Bake at 375° F. for 40 minutes or until pastry is light brown. Serve warm or cold. Makes 6 to 8 servings.

LION HOUSE

Butterscotch Cream Pie

Baked 9-inch pie shell
1⅓ cups sugar
2½ cups milk
¾ cup table cream
5 tablespoons cornstarch
¼ teaspoon salt
3 egg yolks*
1 teaspoon vanilla
2 tablespoons butter or
    margarine
1 cup whipping cream
¼ cup chopped nuts, if
    desired

MEASURE SUGAR INTO A HEAVY saucepan or skillet. Stir constantly over high heat until sugar is nearly melted. Reduce heat to medium and continue stirring until all sugar is melted and a light amber color. In the meantime, heat milk. Stir hot milk into melted sugar cautiously. Sugar will bubble and steam, then harden. Keep heat on low and stir occasionally until the hard sugar completely dissolves in the milk.

In a small bowl add table cream to cornstarch gradually to make a smooth paste, then stir into hot milk mixture. Cook and stir until a smooth, thick pudding is formed. Let it boil a minute or two, stirring vigorously, then remove from heat. Place egg yolks in a small bowl and beat with a fork. Add salt, then stir in some of the hot pudding. Stir egg mixture back into pudding and cook another 2 or 3 minutes. Remove from heat. Add vanilla and butter. Cool 5 minutes, then pour into baked pie shell. Chill 3 to 4 hours. When ready to serve, whip the cream and spread over pie. Sprinkle with nuts. Makes 6 to 8 servings.

*2 whole eggs may be used, but filling may not be as smooth.

LION HOUSE

Pralines and Cream Pie

2 baked 9-inch pie shells
1 quart milk
2 cups half-and-half
2 tablespoons butter
¾ cup sugar
3 egg yolks
½ cup sugar
¼ teaspoon salt
½ cup cornstarch
1½ teaspoons vanilla
¾ cup caramel sauce (ice cream topping)
½ cup chopped pecans*

RESERVE UP TO 1 CUP OF MILK to mix with cornstarch. Place remaining milk in top of a double boiler and add half-and-half, butter, and ¾ cup sugar. Cook until butter is melted and milk looks scalded.

In a bowl, whisk egg yolks until well broken up; then add ½ cup sugar and salt and whisk together very well. Slowly add this mixture to the hot milk mixture, stirring constantly. Stir for approximately ½ minute and then allow to cook for 15 to 20 minutes. (This gives the eggs time to cook and start the thickening process. Undercooking at this point slows the finishing process down by as much as half an hour.)

In a small bowl mix reserved milk and cornstarch together and slowly add to the hot mixture. Be careful to stir constantly or lumps will form. Continue to stir for at least 2 minutes and every 5 minutes for the next 15 to 20 minutes.

A good test to see if the pudding is done enough is to stand up the whisk in the middle of the pudding with the whisk touching the bottom of the pan. If the whisk will stay straight up after you let go, the pudding is thick enough.

When the pudding is thick enough, stir in vanilla. Remove the whole double boiler from stove (the hot water will help keep the pudding hot while you dish up the pies).

Stir caramel sauce and nuts into cream filling. Pour filling into baked pie shells. Fill pies so the tops are a little rounded. When cool, top with whipped cream and drizzle with a little caramel sauce before serving, if desired. Makes 2 pies.

*Walnuts may be substituted.

LION HOUSE

Paradise Isle Pie

2 baked 9-inch pie shells*
1 quart milk
2 cups half-and-half
2 tablespoons butter
¾ cup sugar
3 egg yolks
½ cup sugar
¼ teaspoon salt
½ cup cornstarch
1½ teaspoons vanilla
1 cup coconut, lightly
    measured
1½ cups crushed pineapple,
    slightly drained
1 small can mandarin
    oranges

RESERVE UP TO 1 CUP OF MILK TO mix with cornstarch. Place remaining milk in top of a double boiler and add half-and-half, butter, and ¾ cup sugar. Cook until butter is melted and milk looks scalded.

In a bowl, whisk egg yolks until well broken up; then add ½ cup sugar and salt and whisk together very well. Slowly add this mixture to the hot milk mixture, stirring constantly. Stir for approximately ½ minute and then allow to cook for 15 to 20 minutes. (This gives the eggs time to cook and start the thickening process. Undercooking at this point slows the finishing process down by as much as half an hour.)

Mix reserved milk and cornstarch together and slowly add to the hot mixture. Be careful to stir constantly or lumps will form. Continue to stir for at least 2 minutes and every 5 minutes for the next 15 to 20 minutes.

A good test to see if the pudding is done enough is to stand up the whisk in the middle of the pudding with the whisk touching the bottom of the pan. If the whisk will stay straight up after you let go, the pudding is thick enough.

When the pudding is thick enough, stir in vanilla. Mix in coconut and pineapple. Remove the whole double boiler from stove (the hot water will help keep the pudding hot while you dish up the pies).

Pour hot filling into baked pie shells. Place mandarin oranges around edge of each pie. Makes 2 pies.

*Graham cracker crusts may be substituted.

LION HOUSE

Macadamia Nut Cream Pie

Crust

½ cup butter, softened
¼ cup sugar
¼ teaspoon salt
1 egg yolk
½ teaspoon vanilla
1 cup flour

IN A LARGE BOWL, CREAM TOGETHER butter, sugar, and salt until light and fluffy. Beat in egg yolk and vanilla until well blended. Add flour all at once and beat at low speed just until flour is incorporated. Refrigerate dough at least 1 hour. Roll out dough on a lightly floured surface. Line a 12-inch pie tin with the pastry. Prick dough all around with fork. Bake at 325° F. for 20 minutes or until pastry shell is golden brown.

Filling

1 envelope (1 tablespoon)
    unflavored gelatin
⅓ cup water
3 egg yolks
⅓ cup sugar
1 cup milk
1 cup diced macadamia nuts
½ teaspoon vanilla
1½ cups heavy cream,
    whipped and sweetened

IN A LARGE SAUCEPAN, SPRINKLE gelatin over water; let stand 5 minutes. Place over low heat and cook, stirring constantly, until gelatin dissolves. Remove from heat and set aside. In a small bowl beat egg yolks and sugar until thick and creamy. Heat milk in a medium saucepan to just below boiling point. Remove from heat. Stir 4 tablespoons hot milk into beaten egg yolk mixture. Return egg yolk mixture to milk in saucepan and cook, stirring constantly, until mixture thickens. Remove from heat, stir in macadamia nuts (reserve some for garnish), vanilla, and gelatin in water, and blend thoroughly. Set aside to cool. When cool, fold in whipped cream (reserve some for garnish). Pour filling into baked and cooled pastry shell. Refrigerate 30 minutes. Top with additional whipped cream that has been sweetened to taste with sugar, and garnish with diced macadamia nuts. Serves 10.

LION HOUSE

German Chocolate Cream Pie

2 baked 9-inch pie shells
1 quart milk
2 cups half-and-half
2 tablespoons butter
¾ cup sugar
3 egg yolks
½ cup sugar
¼ teaspoon salt
½ cup cornstarch
1½ teaspoons vanilla
1 cup chocolate chips
1 cup coconut, loosely
   packed
¼ cup caramel sauce (ice
   cream topping)
½ cup chopped pecans*
Whipped cream (optional)

Reserve up to 1 cup of milk to mix with cornstarch. Place remaining milk in top of a double boiler and add half-and-half, butter, and ¾ cup sugar. Cook until butter is melted and milk looks scalded.

In a bowl, whisk egg yolks until well broken up; then add ½ cup sugar and salt and whisk together very well. Slowly add this mixture to the hot milk mixture, stirring constantly. Stir for approximately ½ minute and then allow to cook for 15 to 20 minutes. (This gives the eggs time to cook and start the thickening process. Undercooking at this point slows the finishing process down by as much as half an hour.)

Mix reserved milk and cornstarch together and slowly add to the hot mixture. Be careful to stir constantly or lumps will form. Continue to stir for at least 2 minutes and every 5 minutes for the next 15 to 20 minutes.

A good test to see if the pudding is done enough is to stand up the whisk in the middle of the pudding with the whisk touching the bottom of the pan. If the whisk will stay straight up after you let go, the pudding is thick enough.

When the pudding is thick enough, stir in vanilla. Add chocolate chips and stir until chips are melted. Then add coconut, caramel sauce, and pecans. Remove the whole double boiler from stove (the hot water will help keep the pudding hot while you dish up the pies).

Pour filling into pie shells. Fill pies so the tops are a little rounded. Makes 2 pies. Top with whipped cream, if desired.

Walnuts may be substituted.

Lion House

Chocolate Angel Pie

2 egg whites (room
    temperature)
⅛ teaspoon salt
⅛ teaspoon cream of tartar
½ cup sugar
½ cup finely chopped nuts
½ teaspoon vanilla
1 8-ounce milk chocolate
    bar with almonds
1½ cups heavy cream,
    whipped
1 teaspoon vanilla

PREHEAT OVEN TO 300° F. In a mixer bowl beat egg whites, salt, and cream of tartar till frothy. Add sugar gradually, beating till stiff peaks form. Fold in nuts and vanilla. Spread into greased 9-inch pie pan, building up on sides of pan. Bake for 50 minutes. Cool completely. Break up ¾ of chocolate bar into pieces and melt in top of double boiler or in microwave in glass bowl. When chocolate is just lukewarm, fold it and vanilla into whipped cream. Pile chocolate filling into cooled meringue shell. Grate remaining chocolate to garnish pie. Chill in refrigerator for 2 hours before serving. Makes 6 to 8 servings.

LION HOUSE

Lemonade Chiffon Pie

Baked 9-inch pie shell
1 envelope (1 tablespoon)
    unflavored gelatin
¼ cup cold water
½ cup boiling water
⅔ cup sugar
1 6-ounce can frozen
    lemonade concentrate
1 cup heavy cream, whipped

IN A LARGE SAUCEPAN MIX GELATIN and cold water together. Add boiling water and sugar; stir until dissolved. Add lemonade concentrate; stir until dissolved. Chill until very thick. Fold whipped cream into chilled mixture. Pour into pie shell. Chill. Serve with additional whipped cream, if desired.

LION HOUSE

Lime Chiffon Pie

1 Lite Pie Crust baked pie
   shell
¼ cup sugar
1 envelope unflavored
   gelatin
½ cup water
¼ cup lime juice
2 egg yolks
1 teaspoon finely shredded
   lime peel
1 drop green food coloring,
   if desired
3 egg whites
¼ cup sugar
1 envelope powdered dessert
   topping
½ cup skim milk

In a medium saucepan, combine ¼ cup sugar and gelatin. Add water and lime juice. Cook and stir over low heat until gelatin is completely dissolved. In a medium bowl slightly beat egg yolks. Gradually stir gelatin mixture into egg yolks, then return all of the egg yolk mixture to the saucepan. Bring to a gentle boil; cook and stir 2 minutes more. Remove from heat. Cool slightly. Stir in lime peel and food coloring. Cover and chill until mixture is the consistency of syrup, stirring occasionally.

In a medium bowl, beat the egg whites with an electric mixer on medium speed until soft peaks form. Gradually add ¼ cup sugar, beating on high speed until stiff peaks form. Fold egg whites into slightly thickened gelatin.

Using clean beaters, beat dessert topping with milk according to package directions. Fold whipped topping into gelatin mixture. If necessary, chill the filling until it mounds when spooned (about 1 hour). Spoon the filling into the baked pie shell. Cover and chill at least 4 hours (or overnight, if desired). Makes 8 servings.

Lion House

Almond Coconut Pie

2 chocolate ready crusts

1 quart milk

2 cups half-and-half

2 tablespoons butter

¾ cup sugar

3 egg yolks

½ cup sugar

¼ teaspoon salt

½ cup cornstarch

1½ teaspoons vanilla

1⅔ cups coconut

1⅔ cups almonds, slivered
    and toasted

1½ cups grated chocolate

Whipped cream

RESERVE UP TO 1 CUP OF MILK TO mix with cornstarch. Place remaining milk in top of a double boiler and add half-and-half, butter, and ¾ cup sugar. Cook until butter is melted and milk looks scalded.

In a bowl, whisk egg yolks until well broken up; then add ½ cup sugar and salt and whisk together very well. Slowly add this mixture to the hot milk mixture, stirring constantly. Stir for approximately ½ minute and then allow to cook for 15 to 20 minutes. (This gives the eggs time to cook and start the thickening process. Undercooking at this point slows the finishing process down by as much as half an hour.)

Mix reserved milk and cornstarch together and slowly add to the hot mixture. Be careful to stir constantly or lumps will form. Continue to stir for at least 2 minutes and every 5 minutes for the next 15 to 20 minutes.

A good test to see if the pudding is done enough is to stand up the whisk in the middle of the pudding with the whisk touching the bottom of the pan. If the whisk will stay straight up after you let go, the pudding is thick enough.

When the pudding is thick enough, stir in vanilla. Stir in ⅔ cup coconut and ⅔ cup almonds. Save remaining coconut and almonds for garnish. Remove the whole double boiler from stove (the hot water will help keep the pudding hot while you dish up the pies).

Grate ½ cup chocolate into bottom of pie shells. Set aside remaining grated chocolate for garnish.

Pour filling over grated chocolate in pie shells. Fill pies so the tops are a little rounded. Cool at least 2 hours. Top with whipped cream and garnish with remaining chocolate, coconut, and almonds. Makes 2 pies.

LION HOUSE

Peanut Butter Pie

2 baked 9-inch pie shells
¾ cup peanut butter
1½ cups powdered sugar
1 quart milk
2 cups half-and-half
2 tablespoons butter
¾ cup sugar
3 egg yolks
½ cup sugar
¼ teaspoon salt
½ cup cornstarch
1½ teaspoons vanilla

IN A MEDIUM BOWL MIX together peanut butter and powdered sugar by hand. (This works best when using the same technique as when cutting shortening into flour for pie dough.) Put a thin layer of peanut butter mixture in bottom of baked pie shells. Reserve some for garnishing tops of finished pies.

Reserve up to 1 cup of milk to mix with cornstarch. Place remaining milk in top of a double boiler and add half-and-half, butter, and ¾ cup sugar. Cook until butter is melted and milk looks scalded.

In a bowl, whisk the egg yolks until well broken up; then add ½ cup sugar and salt and whisk together very well. Slowly add this mixture to the hot milk mixture, stirring constantly. Stir for approximately ½ minute and then allow to cook for 15 to 20 minutes. (This gives the eggs time to cook and start the thickening process. Undercooking at this point slows the finishing process down by as much as half an hour.)

Mix reserved milk and cornstarch together and slowly add to the hot mixture. Be careful to stir constantly or lumps will form. Continue to stir for at least 2 minutes and every 5 minutes for the next 15 to 20 minutes.

A good test to see if the pudding is done enough is to stand up the whisk in the middle of the pudding with the whisk touching the bottom of the pan. If the whisk will stay straight up after you let go, the pudding is thick enough.

When the pudding is thick enough, stir in vanilla. Remove the whole double boiler from stove (the hot water will help keep the pudding hot while you dish up the pies).

Pour filling over peanut butter mixture in pie shells. Fill pies so the tops are a little rounded. Sprinkle reserved peanut butter filling on top. Gently pat the mixture so it doesn't fall off when serving. Chill well. Makes 2 pies.

LION HOUSE

CHOCOLATE CRACKLE COOKIES. RECIPE ON PAGE 101.
RUBY'S PEANUT BUTTER COOKIES. RECIPE ON PAGE 106.

CHAPTER FOUR
Cookies
& Bars

Chocolate Crackle Cookies

¼ cup shortening, melted
¼ cup cocoa
½ cup oil
2 cups sugar
4 eggs
2 teaspoons vanilla
2½ cups flour
½ teaspoon salt
1½ teaspoons baking powder
½ cup walnuts, chopped
½ cup chocolate chips
    (optional)
½ to 1 cup powdered sugar

PREHEAT OVEN TO 350° F. In a large mixing bowl, cream together shortening, cocoa, oil, sugar, eggs, and vanilla until well mixed. Add flour, salt, and baking powder. Mix well, then add walnuts and chocolate chips, if desired. (Dough will be very sticky and almost runny.) Refrigerate dough for 2 to 3 hours or overnight. Drop and gently roll dough by table-spoonfuls in powdered sugar, being careful not to overhandle dough. Place on a greased or wax paper—covered cookie sheet. Bake for 9 to 10 minutes. Do not overbake. The cookie dough may be stored in the refrigerator for up to 5 days; baked cookies will store for at least 2 weeks, if well covered and refrigerated. These cookies freeze beautifully. Makes approximately 5 dozen cookies.

LION HOUSE

Pictured on page 98.

Chocolate Chip Cookies

1¾ cups softened butter
1¾ cups brown sugar
1¼ cups granulated sugar
4 eggs
5½ tablespoons water
1½ teaspoons vanilla
6 cups all-purpose flour
1½ teaspoons salt
1½ teaspoons soda
3 cups chocolate chips

PREHEAT OVEN TO 350° F. Line a cookie sheet with wax paper. Set aside. In a large mixing bowl, cream butter and sugars. Add eggs, water, and vanilla and mix until creamy. Add the flour, salt, and soda. Mix well. Gently fold in chocolate chips, mixing only until chips are evenly distributed. (Overmixing results in broken chips and discolored dough.) Drop by spoonfuls onto prepared cookie sheet. Bake for 8 to 10 minutes or until golden brown. Makes 5 to 6 dozen 3½-inch cookies.

LION HOUSE

Pumpkin Chocolate Chip Cookies

¾ cup granulated sugar

¾ cup brown sugar

3½ teaspoons pumpkin pie
    spice

1½ cups pumpkin, canned

¾ cup oil

7 eggs

2 teaspoons baking soda

2 teaspoons baking powder

¾ teaspoon salt

4½ cups pastry flour

1½ cups chocolate chips

1¼ cups walnuts, chopped

PREHEAT OVEN TO 350° F. In a large mixer bowl mix together sugars, pumpkin pie spice, pumpkin, oil, and eggs until well blended. In a separate bowl, blend baking soda, baking powder, salt, and flour; combine with pumpkin mix. Mix together until well blended, then add chocolate chips and walnuts. Drop by spoonfuls on a cookie sheet lined with wax paper or a well-greased pan. Bake for 8 minutes. Makes 5 dozen cookies.

Note: These cookies may be frozen and stored for later.

LION HOUSE

Sugar Cookies

1½ cups sugar

⅔ cup butter or shortening*

2 eggs, beaten

2 tablespoons milk

1 teaspoon vanilla

3¼ cups flour

2½ teaspoons baking powder

½ teaspoon salt

Decorative toppings
    (optional)

IN A LARGE MIXER BOWL CREAM sugar and butter. Add eggs, milk, and vanilla. Sift flour, baking powder, and salt together and beat into creamed mixture, combining thoroughly. With hands, shape dough into a ball; wrap and refrigerate 2 to 3 hours (or overnight) until easy to handle.

Grease cookie sheets lightly. On lightly floured board, roll one-half or one-third of the dough at a time, keeping the rest refrigerated. For crisp cookies, roll dough paper-thin. For softer cookies, roll ⅛-inch to ¼-inch thick. Cut into desired shapes with a floured cookie cutter. Reroll trimmings and cut.

Place cookies one-half inch apart on cookie sheets. Sprinkle with decorative toppings, if desired. Bake at 350° F. about 8 minutes or until a very light brown. Remove cookies to racks to cool. Makes about 6 dozen cookies.

Decorative Toppings: Brush cookies with heavy cream or with a mixture of one egg white slightly beaten with one tablespoon water. Sprinkle with sugar, nonpareils, chopped nuts, shredded coconut, cut-up gumdrops, or butterscotch pieces.

Butter makes a better-tasting cookie.

LION HOUSE

Cutout Sugar Cookies

2 cups granulated sugar

1 cup shortening

3 eggs

1 cup milk

1 teaspoon vanilla

1 teaspoon lemon extract

6½ cups all-purpose flour

1 teaspoon salt

1 teaspoon soda

3½ teaspoons baking powder

Butter Cream Icing

¾ cup butter

¾ cup shortening

4⅔ cups powdered sugar

1½ teaspoons lemon juice

1½ teaspoons vanilla

⅓ cup water

PREHEAT OVEN TO 350° F. LINE A cookie sheet with wax paper and set aside. In a large mixer bowl cream together sugar, shortening, and eggs. Add milk, vanilla, and lemon extract; mix at low speed. In a separate bowl, mix flour, salt, soda, and baking powder. Add to the sugar mixture until well incorporated. Roll out ⅛-inch thick; cut out in desired shapes. Bake for 6 minutes, being careful not to overbake. Cookies should be light golden brown around the edges. Frost with Butter Cream Icing. Makes 5 to 6 dozen cookies.

IN A LARGE MIXER BOWL COMBINE butter, shortening, and sugar and beat until very creamy. Add lemon juice and vanilla. Mix until well blended. Add water and mix until very light.

LION HOUSE

Snickerdoodles

½ cup granulated sugar

1¼ teaspoons cinnamon

1 cup butter, softened

2½ cups sugar

4 eggs

1 teaspoon vanilla

2½ tablespoons water

6 cups all-purpose flour

2 teaspoons cream of tartar

1 teaspoon soda

½ teaspoon salt

PREHEAT OVEN TO 350° F. Mix ½ cup sugar and cinnamon together in a medium bowl and set aside. In a large mixing bowl, combine butter and 2½ cups sugar until light and fluffy. Add eggs, vanilla, and water; beat until fluffy. Add flour, cream of tartar, soda, and salt, turning the mixer on and off in quick bursts at low speed until the flour is mostly incorporated. Continue mixing at medium speed until well mixed. Drop cookies by rounded tablespoonfuls into cinnamon-sugar mixture. Roll the dough around until it is completely covered. Place on a cookie sheet lined with wax paper and bake for 9 to 10 minutes or until golden brown. Makes 5 dozen 3-inch cookies.

LION HOUSE

Oatmeal Raisin Cookies

2 cups boiling water

2 cups raisins

3 cups sugar

1½ cups shortening

4 eggs

1 cup raisin liquid

2 teaspoons vanilla

5 cups flour

1 teaspoon baking powder

2 teaspoons soda

2 teaspoons salt

2 teaspoons cinnamon

2 teaspoons cloves

4 cups quick oats

Preheat oven to 350° F. Bring 2 cups of water to a boil in a medium saucepan. Add raisins to boiling water. Set aside.

In a large mixing bowl cream sugar and shortening until fluffy. Stir in eggs one at a time. Strain raisins from liquid and add 1 cup of liquid to the sugar and shortening mixture. Add vanilla. Mix until well blended. Discard remaining liquid. In a separate bowl, mix together flour, baking powder, soda, salt, cinnamon, cloves, and oats. Add to the creamed mixture. (This may require hand mixing.)

Carefully stir in the raisins. Scoop walnut-sized scoops onto ungreased cookie sheets and bake for 12 minutes. Makes approximately 12 dozen cookies.

Joseph Smith Building

Cookies
& Bars

Oatmeal Cookies

1 cup brown sugar

1 cup granulated sugar

1 cup butter, softened

4 eggs

2 teaspoons vanilla

2¼ cups all-purpose flour

1 teaspoon soda

½ teaspoon salt

2½ cups oatmeal

1 cup raisins

Preheat oven to 350° F. Grease a cookie sheet or line with wax paper. In a large mixing bowl, cream sugars and butter. Add eggs and vanilla. Mix in flour, soda, salt, oatmeal, and raisins. Drop by large rounded tablespoonfuls onto a greased or lined cookie sheet. Bake for 8 to 9 minutes. Makes 2½ dozen cookies.

Lion House

Oatmeal Scotchies

1 cup butter

1½ cups brown sugar

2 eggs

1 tablespoon water

2 cups all-purpose flour

2 teaspoons baking powder

1 teaspoon soda

1 teaspoon salt

1½ cups oatmeal

¾ teaspoon orange extract

1½ cups butterscotch chips

PREHEAT OVEN TO 350° F. GREASE a cookie sheet or line with wax paper. Set aside. In a large mixing bowl, combine butter and sugar and mix until creamy. Add eggs and water and beat until smooth. Mix flour, baking powder, soda, and salt together in a separate bowl. Add to mixture in mixer bowl and mix well. Then add oatmeal, orange extract, and butterscotch chips. Mix until just blended. Drop by rounded teaspoonfuls onto prepared cookie sheet. Bake for 8 to 10 minutes.

Variation: Substitute vanilla for the orange extract and chocolate chips for the butterscotch chips.

LION HOUSE

Thora's Butterscotch Cookies

½ cup butter or margarine

1½ cups brown sugar

2 eggs

1 teaspoon vanilla

2⅔ cups flour

1 teaspoon baking soda

½ teaspoon baking powder

½ teaspoon salt

1 cup sour cream

1 cup chopped pecans

Frosting

½ cup butter

3 cups powdered sugar

¼ cup hot water

Pecan halves

PREHEAT OVEN TO 350° F. GREASE a cookie sheet and set aside. Cream butter and brown sugar in a large mixer bowl; add eggs and vanilla and beat well. Sift flour, baking soda, baking powder, and salt, and add to creamed mixture alternately with sour cream. Fold in chopped nuts. Drop by spoonfuls onto greased cookie sheet. Bake for 10 minutes. Cool on wire rack.

COOK BUTTER IN SAUCEPAN over medium heat till bubbly and golden brown. Beat in powdered sugar and hot water. Frost cooled cookies and top each with a pecan half. Store in covered container. Makes 5 dozen cookies.

LION HOUSE

Peanut Butter Cookies

5¼ cups all-purpose flour
2 teaspoons soda
1 teaspoon salt
1 cup butter
¾ cup shortening
1¾ cups sugar
1¾ cups brown sugar
4 eggs
1 teaspoon vanilla
¾ cup peanut butter

PREHEAT OVEN TO 350° F. Line a cookie sheet with wax paper and set aside. Mix flour, soda, and salt together in a medium bowl and set aside. Cream together butter, shortening, sugar, brown sugar, eggs, and vanilla in a large mixing bowl. Then stir in peanut butter. Add flour mixture and stir until well blended. Drop dough by tablespoonfuls onto cookie sheet. Using a fork dipped in flour, flatten each cookie slightly in a crisscross pattern. Bake for 8 to 10 minutes or until slightly golden around the edges. Do not overbake. Makes 5 dozen 3-inch cookies.

LION HOUSE

Ruby's Peanut Butter Cookies

1 cup sugar
1 cup brown sugar
1 cup shortening
1 cup peanut butter
1 teaspoon salt
1 teaspoon vanilla
2 eggs
¼ cup milk
3½ cups flour
2 teaspoons soda

PREHEAT OVEN TO 350° F. Line a cookie sheet with wax paper. Set aside. In a large mixing bowl, combine sugars, shortening, peanut butter, salt, and vanilla. Mix well. Add alternately eggs and milk; mix until creamy. Fold in flour and soda. Transfer the dough to a clean, flat surface and do the final mixing by hand. Drop by rounded teaspoonfuls or roll into walnut-sized balls and place on prepared cookie sheet. Flatten with a fork or the bottom of a glass dipped in sugar. Bake for 8 to 10 minutes.

Variation: For a flower cookie, press a Hershey Kiss® into each cookie as soon as cookies are removed from oven. Makes 5 dozen cookies.

JOSEPH SMITH BUILDING

Pictured on page 98.

Date Pinwheels

Filling

2 cups chopped dates

1 cup sugar

1 cup water

1 cup chopped nuts

To MAKE FILLING: MIX DATES, sugar, and water together in small saucepan and cook 10 minutes. Mix in nuts and cool.

Cookies

1 cup margarine

2 cups brown sugar

3 eggs

4 cups flour

½ teaspoon salt

½ teaspoon baking soda

To MAKE COOKIES: In a large mixing bowl, cream margarine and brown sugar. Beat in eggs. Sift together flour, salt, and baking soda; stir into creamed mixture (dough will be stiff). Divide dough in half; chill 1 hour or till dough can be rolled easily. On lightly floured surface, roll dough out into two 10x15-inch rectangles.

Spread each rectangle with half of date filling. Carefully roll up jelly-roll style, beginning at long side. Wrap each roll in wax paper and refrigerate several hours. Cut into ¼-inch slices. Place on greased cookie sheet. Bake at 375° F. for about 12 minutes. Remove from cookie sheet and cool on wire rack. Store in covered container. Makes 6 dozen cookies.

LION HOUSE

Myrtle's Icebox Date Cookies

1 cup butter

2 cups brown sugar

2 eggs

2 teaspoons vanilla

4½ cups all-purpose flour

1 teaspoon soda

1 cup chopped dates

1 cup chopped pecans or
    other nuts, if desired

PREHEAT OVEN TO 350° F. Cream butter and sugar in a large mixing bowl. Add eggs and vanilla and mix well. Add flour and soda and blend until incorporated. Then add dates and nuts and mix well. Divide dough into 3 or 4 equal parts and roll into logs. Wrap each log in wax paper and refrigerate for 24 hours. Or scoop into balls and press down while dough is still fresh. If using the refrigerator method, cut into slices while still cold. Bake on a lined cookie sheet for 10 to 15 minutes. Be careful not to overbake. For best results, take cookies out of the oven before they're completely done and leave on hot cookie sheet a few minutes to finish baking.

LION HOUSE

Janell's Mock Turtle Cookies

Pecans, chopped
½ cup butter
1 cup brown sugar
2 eggs
2 egg yolks
1 teaspoon vanilla
¾ teaspoon maple flavoring
3 cups all-purpose flour
½ teaspoon salt
½ teaspoon soda

PREHEAT OVEN TO 350° F. Chop pecans, place in bowl, and set aside. In a large mixing bowl, cream butter and sugar. Add eggs, egg yolks, vanilla, and maple flavoring and mix well. Add flour, salt, and soda and mix well. Drop rounded tablespoonfuls into chopped pecans; gently press down. (The nuts need to be stuck in the dough of the bottom of the cookie.) Place, with the nuts down, on cookie sheet lined with wax paper. Bake for 10 to 12 minutes or until slightly golden around the edges. When cookies are cool, spread with Chocolate Icing. Makes 2 to 3 dozen 3-inch cookies.

Chocolate Icing
2 tablespoons butter
3 tablespoons cocoa
1½ cups powdered sugar
¼ cup evaporated milk

CREAM BUTTER AND COCOA together in a small mixing bowl. Add powdered sugar and half of the milk; mix on low speed. Slowly add the rest of the milk. Beat until well blended.

LION HOUSE

Layered Cookies

½ cup butter or margarine
1 cup graham cracker
    crumbs
1 cup coconut
1 cup chocolate chips
1 cup butterscotch chips
1 cup chopped nuts
1 can sweetened condensed
    milk

PREHEAT OVEN TO 350° F. MELT butter in a 9x13-inch pan. Sprinkle over the butter, in layers, graham cracker crumbs, then coconut, then chocolate chips, then butterscotch chips, then nuts. Drizzle with sweetened condensed milk. Bake for 30 minutes. Cut away from sides of pan when you take from oven. Cut in squares while still warm.

LION HOUSE

Black-and-White Biscotti

3 cups flour

½ cup sugar

½ cup brown sugar

3 teaspoons baking powder

½ teaspoon salt

4 ounces unsweetened
    chocolate, melted

1 teaspoon grated orange
    peel

⅓ cup olive oil

¼ cup orange juice

2 teaspoons vanilla

3 eggs

6 ounces white chocolate,
    chopped

PREHEAT OVEN TO 350° F. Lightly grease 2 baking sheets; set aside. Stir together flour, sugar, brown sugar, baking powder, and salt in a large bowl. Add melted chocolate, orange peel, oil, orange juice, vanilla, and eggs. Blend well to make a stiff dough. Knead chopped white chocolate into dough. Divide dough into 4 equal parts; shape each part into a log about 14 inches long. Place 2 logs on each baking sheet; flatten with fingers to a width of about 2½ inches each. Bake in preheated oven for 18 to 20 minutes or until firm to the touch.

Remove baking sheets from oven. Reduce oven temperature to 300° F. Cool logs on baking sheets for 10 minutes. Cut warm logs diagonally into ½-inch-wide slices. Place slices, cut side up, on same baking sheets. Bake at 300° F. for 7 to 9 minutes or until top surface is dry. Turn cookies over and bake an additional 7 to 9 minutes. Remove cookies from sheets and cool completely on wire racks.

Topping

4 ounces white chocolate,
    chopped

1 tablespoon shortening

MELT WHITE CHOCOLATE WITH SHORTENING in a small saucepan over low heat, stirring until smooth. Drizzle over cookies. Biscotti can be stored in an airtight container for up to 4 weeks. Makes 7 dozen.

LION HOUSE

Filled Cookies

Raisin Filling

2 cups raisins

¾ cup water

¾ cup sugar

¼ cup cornstarch, well
    rounded

½ teaspoon vanilla

1 tablespoon butter

To MAKE RAISIN FILLING: In a medium saucepan, combine raisins and water, allow to boil for 10 minutes. In a separate bowl, mix sugar and cornstarch together until well blended. Slowly pour this mixture into the boiling raisins, stirring constantly. Continue stirring for another 10 to 15 minutes until sauce is thickened and there is no starchy taste. Remove from heat; add vanilla and butter and stir until the butter is melted. Allow mixture to cool before filling the cookies.

Cookies

1 cup margarine

2 cups sugar

½ cup minus 1 tablespoon
    honey

1 teaspoon salt

1 teaspoon soda

2 eggs

7 cups pastry flour

1 tablespoon cream of tartar

¼ cup water

To MAKE COOKIES: Preheat oven to 350° F. In a large mixing bowl, combine margarine, sugar, honey, salt, and soda. Then add eggs and mix together on low speed until smooth. Add flour, cream of tartar, and water; increase speed to medium. Then beat on medium high and continue blending until all ingredients are well combined.

Grease a cookie sheet or line with wax paper and set aside. On a lightly floured board using a floured rolling pin, roll out dough. With a large round cookie cutter, cut dough into circles. Place 1 teaspoon to 1 tablespoon of raisin filling along the middle of the cookie and fold in half.* Bake for 9 to 10 minutes or until cookies are slightly golden around the edges. Do not overbake.

Note: This is a great recipe to use up hardened raisins. Fresh raisins have an enzyme that will not allow the cornstarch to thicken. If all you have is fresh (soft) raisins, it is best to spread them out in a thin layer on a cookie sheet and leave them out to dry in a warm place for several days. You can also put them on a cookie sheet and place in a warm oven (not over 200°) for about an hour.

*The amount of filling will vary depending on the size of the cookie. Baking time will also vary.

LION HOUSE

Applesauce Cookies

1 cup butter
2½ cups brown sugar
4 eggs
2 teaspoons vanilla
1½ cups applesauce
5½ cups all-purpose flour
2 teaspoons soda
1½ teaspoons salt
1½ teaspoons cloves
2 cups raisins (optional)

PREHEAT OVEN TO 350° F. In a large mixing bowl, cream together butter and sugar. Add eggs and vanilla and beat until light and fluffy. Mix in applesauce, then add flour, soda, salt, and cloves. Add raisins, if desired. Mix all ingredients together, making sure to scrape the sides of bowl. Drop by rounded tablespoonfuls onto a cookie sheet lined with wax paper. Bake for 8 to 10 minutes or until lightly browned at the edges.

Frost with Almond Cream Cheese Icing while cookies are still warm. Makes 5 dozen cookies.

Almond Cream Cheese Icing

¼ cup butter
1 8-ounce package cream cheese, softened
2½ cups powdered sugar
1 tablespoon milk
2 teaspoons almond extract

CREAM BUTTER AND CREAM CHEESE together in a medium mixing bowl. Add powdered sugar, milk, and almond extract; mix well.

LION HOUSE

Raspberry Sticks

1 cup butter
¾ cup sugar
1 egg
1 teaspoon vanilla
2½ cups flour
¼ teaspoon salt
1 to 2 tablespoons water (if needed)
Raspberry jam

IN A LARGE MIXER BOWL, cream butter and sugar together until light and fluffy. Add egg and vanilla; beat well. Sift flour and salt together; add to creamed mixture a third at a time, mixing well after each addition. If dough is too stiff, add 1 or 2 tablespoons water. Wrap dough in plastic wrap and chill in refrigerator for about 1 hour.

Preheat oven to 375° F. Cut the chilled dough into 4 pieces. Roll each piece into a rope the length of your cookie sheet. Put ropes onto the cookie sheet, side by side. With your finger, make an indentation all the way down the length of each rope. Bake in preheated oven for 6 minutes. Remove from oven and fill the indentation with raspberry jam. Put back into the oven for another 6 to 8 minutes. Place cookie sheet on rack to cool cookies. Cut on the diagonal. Makes 3 dozen.

LION HOUSE

Carrot Cookies

1½ cups butter, softened

1½ cups sugar

1 egg

3 cups carrots, finely grated

3¾ cups all-purpose flour

½ teaspoon salt

½ tablespoon baking powder

½ to 1 tablespoon grated
    orange rind

PREHEAT OVEN TO 350° F. In a large mixing bowl, cream together butter and sugar, then add egg and carrots. Mix well, then add flour, salt, baking powder, and orange rind. Beat until well mixed. Drop by spoonfuls onto a greased cookie sheet. Bake for 12 minutes. Cool and frost with Orange Icing. Makes 5 dozen cookies.

Orange Icing

3⅓ cups powdered sugar

⅓ cup plus 2 tablespoons
    heavy whipping cream

1 teaspoon orange extract

½ teaspoon vanilla

1 tablespoon grated orange
    rind (approximately 2
    oranges)

1 tablespoon orange juice
    (use juice from the 2
    grated oranges)

MIX ALL INGREDIENTS TOGETHER IN a mixing bowl until smooth. Spread lightly on carrot cookies.

LION HOUSE

Sour Cream Cookies

1 cup butter, softened

1⅓ cups sugar

2 eggs

2 teaspoons vanilla

1 cup sour cream

6 cups all-purpose flour

1½ teaspoons soda

1 teaspoon salt

1 cup pineapple, well
    drained

PREHEAT OVEN 350° F. In a large mixer bowl, blend butter, sugar, eggs, and vanilla. Fold in sour cream; mix on low speed. Add flour, soda, and salt and mix until all ingredients are combined. Drain pineapple and reserve liquid for frosting. Stir in pineapple until just mixed. Drop cookies by rounded tablespoonfuls onto a greased cookie sheet and bake for 12 minutes. Frost with Pineapple Cream Cheese Frosting. Makes 5 dozen 2½-inch cookies.

Variation: To make lemon sour cream cookies, substitute 1½ teaspoons lemon extract and 1½ teaspoons lemon zest for pineapple. Frost with Lemon Cream Cheese Frosting.

Pineapple Cream Cheese Frosting

1 3-ounce package cream
    cheese, softened

¼ cup margarine

3 cups powdered sugar

1 teaspoon vanilla

1 to 3 tablespoons pineapple
    juice

WHIP CREAM CHEESE AND MARGARINE in a large mixer bowl; add powdered sugar and vanilla. Add pineapple juice and mix until smooth. Add more pineapple juice if needed to reach desired spreading consistency.

Lemon Cream Cheese Frosting

1 3-ounce package cream
    cheese, softened

¼ cup margarine

3 cups powdered sugar

1 teaspoon vanilla

1 to 3 tablespoons lemon
    juice

1 tablespoon lemon zest

WHIP CREAM CHEESE AND MARGARINE in a large mixer bowl; add powdered sugar and vanilla. Add lemon juice and lemon zest and mix until smooth. Add more lemon juice if needed to reach desired spreading consistency.

LION HOUSE

Macadamia White Chocolate Cookies

1 cup butter, softened

1 cup shortening

1½ cups granulated sugar

1½ cups brown sugar

1 teaspoon vanilla

4 eggs

4 to 4¼ cups flour

2 teaspoons salt

2 teaspoons soda

1 cup quick oats

1 cup macadamia nuts, chopped*

2 cups (one 12-ounce package) white chocolate chips*

PREHEAT OVEN TO 350° F. Cream butter, shortening, and sugars until light and fluffy in a large mixing bowl. Add vanilla and eggs one at a time.

In a separate bowl, mix together flour, salt, soda, and oats. Add flour mixture to creamed mixture and blend until incorporated. Fold in nuts and chips by hand, unless you have a heavy-duty mixer.

Drop walnut-sized balls of dough onto an ungreased cookie sheet. Bake for 12 to 15 minutes or until edges are light golden brown. Makes 5 dozen cookies.

Chocolate chips may be substituted for white chocolate chips. If substituting chocolate chips, use walnuts or pecans in place of macadamia nuts.

JOSEPH SMITH BUILDING

Ginger Cookies

½ cup granulated sugar

½ cup brown sugar

¾ cup shortening

¼ cup molasses

1 egg

2 cups all-purpose flour

2 teaspoons soda

¼ teaspoon salt

1 teaspoon cinnamon

1½ teaspoons ginger

PREHEAT OVEN TO 350° F. In a large mixing bowl, combine sugars and shortening until mixture is light and fluffy. Add molasses and egg; beat well. Add flour, soda, salt, cinnamon, and ginger and beat well. Scrape down the sides of bowl, then mix again. Drop dough by rounded tablespoonfuls onto a lightly greased cookie sheet. Press down each cookie with the bottom of a glass dipped in sugar. Bake for 8 to 10 minutes, being careful not to overbake.

Note: These cookies are used as children's birthday party cookies at the Lion House.

LION HOUSE

Martha's Molasses Cookies

¾ cup shortening

1¼ cups sugar

¼ cup molasses

1 egg

3½ cups all-purpose flour*

    ¾ teaspoon salt

1½ teaspoons soda

½ teaspoon cloves

½ teaspoon nutmeg

2 teaspoons cinnamon

2 teaspoons ginger

1 cup sour milk or buttermilk

2 cups pecans, chopped
(optional)

2 cups raisins (optional)

PREHEAT OVEN TO 350° F. In a large mixing bowl cream together the shortening, sugar, and molasses. Add egg and mix well. Add flour, salt, soda, cloves, nutmeg, cinnamon, and ginger; blend at low speed until just mixed. Slowly add milk or buttermilk and mix on low speed. Add nuts or raisins (or half of each) if desired. Drop by rounded tablespoonfuls on a cookie sheet lined with wax paper. Bake for 10 to 12 minutes or until cookies are slightly brown around the edges. Serve plain or frost with Butter Cream Icing. Makes 4 to 5 dozen cookies.

*Amount of flour may vary.

Butter Cream Icing

3 cups powdered sugar

½ cup butter

6 to 8 tablespoons cream or
evaporated milk

1 teaspoon vanilla

PLACE POWDERED SUGAR IN A mixing bowl. Add butter and 3 tablespoons of the cream. Blend on low speed until mixed. Slowly add the rest of the cream, 1 tablespoon at a time, until creamy and smooth, but not at all runny. Add vanilla and mix again.

LION HOUSE

Ginger Chews

⅓ cup light butter, softened

⅔ cup firmly packed brown
    sugar

1 teaspoon baking soda

1 teaspoon ginger

½ teaspoon cinnamon

1 egg

¼ cup dark molasses

1½ cups white flour

½ cup whole wheat flour

¼ cup granulated sugar

1 teaspoon cinnamon

SPRAY COOKIE SHEET WITH NONSTICK cooking spray; set aside. In a large mixing bowl, beat butter with an electric mixer on medium to high speed for 30 seconds. Add brown sugar, baking soda, ginger, and ½ teaspoon cinnamon; beat until combined. Beat in egg and molasses. Beat in as much of the white and whole wheat flours as you can with the mixer. Stir in any remaining flour with a wooden spoon. Cover and chill in the refrigerator for 1 hour.

Shape dough into 1-inch balls. Combine the granulated sugar and 1 teaspoon cinnamon. Roll balls in sugar-cinnamon mixture. Place 2 inches apart on prepared cookie sheet. Bake at 350° F. for 10 to 11 minutes or until tops of cookies are cracked. (Cookies are best if slightly underbaked.) Remove from cookie sheet and cool on wire racks. Makes about 4 dozen cookies.

LION HOUSE

Cookies
& Bars

Coconut Chews

½ cup butter

1 cup flour

2 tablespoons sugar

Pinch salt

1½ cups brown sugar

2 eggs

2 teaspoons vanilla

1 cup flaked coconut

1 cup chopped nuts

IN A MEDIUM BOWL CUT BUTTER into flour, sugar, and salt with pastry blender. Press into 8x12-inch baking pan. Bake at 350° F. for 15 minutes.

Beat brown sugar and eggs together in mixer bowl till smooth. Add vanilla, coconut, and nuts. Carefully spread over baked crust, then return to oven and continue baking for 25 minutes longer. Cut into squares while warm. Cool, then cover pan to store. Makes 24 bars.

LION HOUSE

Rich Chocolate Nut Cookies

1 cup butter
1 cup sugar
1 cup brown sugar
2 eggs
3¼ cups oatmeal
2 cups flour
½ teaspoon salt
1 teaspoon baking powder
1 teaspoon soda
1 teaspoon vanilla
1½ cups walnuts, chopped
12 ounces semisweet chocolate chips
4 ounces Hershey® bar,
   grated

PREHEAT OVEN TO 350° F. In a large mixing bowl, combine butter and sugars. Add eggs and beat until light and fluffy. Blend
the 3¼ cups oatmeal in a blender. This should measure 2½
cups after blending. In a separate bowl, mix together flour,
salt, baking powder, soda, and vanilla. Add oatmeal. Stir in
nuts, chocolate chips, and grated Hershey bar until all
ingredients are well blended. Drop by rounded tablespoonfuls onto cookie sheet lined with wax paper and bake for
10 minutes, or until slightly brown at the edges.

LION HOUSE

Peanut Butter Fingers

½ cup butter or margarine
½ cup white sugar
½ cup brown sugar
1 egg
⅓ cup peanut butter
½ teaspoon baking soda
¼ teaspoon salt
½ teaspoon vanilla
1 cup flour
1 cup quick-cooking oats
½ cup sifted powdered sugar
¼ cup peanut butter
1 to 2 tablespoons milk
1 6-ounce package chocolate
   chips

PREHEAT OVEN TO 350° F. GREASE a 9x13x2-inch baking pan
and set aside. In a large mixer bowl cream butter and sugars.
Blend in egg, ⅓ cup peanut butter, baking soda, salt, and
vanilla. Stir in flour and oats. Pour into prepared baking pan
and bake in preheated oven for 20 to 25 minutes.

While bars are cooking, prepare peanut butter frosting by
creaming together powdered sugar, ¼ cup peanut butter, and
enough milk to make mixture desired spreading consistency.
Set aside.

When bars are done remove pan from oven and sprinkle
with chocolate chips. Let stand 5 minutes, then spread the
melted chips like frosting. With knife or spatula, swirl peanut
butter frosting over chocolate frosting. Cool thoroughly,
then cut into 24 bars.

LION HOUSE

Gene's Chocolate Sandwich Cookies

6 tablespoons raisins

1 cup nuts

1 cup sugar

½ cup shortening

2 teaspoons corn syrup

6 tablespoons cocoa

1½ teaspoons salt

3 eggs

½ teaspoon vanilla

1¾ cups all-purpose flour

To make cookies: Preheat oven to 350° F. Mix raisins and nuts together and grind in a blender until very fine. Set aside. In a large mixing bowl, cream sugar and shortening until light and fluffy. Add corn syrup, cocoa, salt, eggs, and vanilla; mix well. Add nut and raisin mixture and flour. Mix well.

Drop by rounded teaspoonfuls on wax paper—lined or well-greased cookie sheet. Bake for 8 to 10 minutes. Spread Mint Butter Cream Icing on the flat side of one cookie and place the flat side of a second cookie on top of the icing. Drizzle Chocolate Ganache on the top of the second cookie. Makes 30 cookies.

Mint Butter Cream Icing

3 cups powdered sugar

½ cup butter

6 to 8 tablespoons cream or evaporated milk

1 teaspoon vanilla

¼ teaspoon mint flavoring

1 to 2 drops green food coloring

To make mint butter cream icing: Place powdered sugar in a mixing bowl. Add butter and 3 tablespoons of the cream. Blend on low speed until mixed. Slowly add the rest of the cream, 1 tablespoon at a time, until creamy and smooth, but not at all runny. Add vanilla, mint flavoring, and food coloring and mix again.

Chocolate Ganache

½ cup heavy whipping cream

2 teaspoons butter

1 cup semisweet chocolate chips

2 or 3 drops imitation rum flavoring

To make chocolate ganache: Pour cream into a saucepan and boil for 1 minute, stirring constantly. Remove from heat and add butter, chocolate chips, and flavoring and stir until completely melted and smooth.

If mixture gets too thick to use, return it to medium heat on stove and reheat, stirring constantly.

Note: Chocolate Ganache may be used as eclair icing.

Lion House

Toffee Bars

1½ cups butter

1 cup plus 2 tablespoons sugar

¼ teaspoon salt

2 eggs

1 teaspoon vanilla

4⅔ cups all-purpose flour

2 to 3 tablespoons water, if needed

2 cups toffee bar chips or crushed Heath Bars®

15 Hershey® bars (1.55-ounces each)

Preheat oven to 375° F. In a large mixing bowl, cream butter, sugar, and salt together until light and fluffy. Add eggs and vanilla; beat well. Measure flour and add to the mixture one-third at a time, beating well after each addition. If the dough is too stiff, add 2 to 3 tablespoons water and mix well. Spread evenly in a 12x15-inch jelly roll pan. Prick with a fork at about 2-inch intervals, then bake for 12 to 15 minutes or until the bars are light golden brown. Remove from oven and sprinkle with 1 cup of the toffee chips, then set unwrapped Hershey bar(s) on top of the chips. (The heat from the bars will melt the toffee chips and chocolate.) Slightly spread the chocolate as it melts, then cut the bars into 3-inch squares. Cut each bar diagonally into triangles. Allow to cool slightly, then sprinkle remaining toffee chips over the bars. Makes 40 small triangle-shaped bars.

Lion House

Banana Bars

1 cup butter, softened

2 cups sugar

4 eggs

4 ripe bananas, mashed

2 teaspoons lemon juice

3 cups all-purpose flour

1 teaspoon salt

1 teaspoon soda

½ cup buttermilk

1 cup nuts, chopped (optional)

Preheat oven to 350° F. In a large mixing bowl, cream sugar and butter until smooth. Add eggs and bananas and beat until smooth. Add lemon juice and mix briefly. Mix flour, salt, and soda together in a separate bowl; add to creamed mixture alternately with buttermilk. Fold in nuts with the last addition of buttermilk. Do not overmix. Pour into a greased and floured jelly-roll pan (17½x12½). Bake for 30 minutes. Allow to cool, then frost with Peter Pan Icing. Makes 2 dozen 2x2-inch bars.

Note: Banana Bars taste even better the second day.

Peter Pan Icing

1 cup butter

1 egg

5 cups powdered sugar

1⅓ tablespoons half-and-half or evaporated milk

In a large mixing bowl, beat butter until smooth. (This works best if butter is cold). Add egg and powdered sugar and beat just until combined. Add half-and-half or evaporated milk; beat until smooth and creamy. Spread on bars.

Note: This makes more frosting than needed, but half of the recipe is not enough. Frosting will keep for a long time if refrigerated.

Lion House

Date Bars with Orange Icing

1 cup flour
1 teaspoon baking powder
½ teaspoon cinnamon
¼ teaspoon baking soda
½ cup snipped dates
1 cup boiling water
2 eggs
1 cup firmly packed brown
  sugar
¾ cup evaporated skim milk
¼ cup finely chopped
  toasted walnuts
2 cups confectioner's sugar
2 tablespoons light butter,
  softened
2 tablespoons orange juice
½ teaspoon finely shredded
  orange peel

PREHEAT OVEN TO 350° F. Spray a 13x9-inch baking pan with nonstick cooking spray; set aside.

Stir or sift together flour, baking powder, cinnamon, and baking soda. Set aside.

Place dates in a small bowl and pour boiling water over them. Let stand for 10 minutes. Drain well. In a large mixing bowl, beat eggs with an electric mixer on high speed until frothy. Add brown sugar and dates, beating until mixture is well combined. Stir in evaporated skim milk.

Add flour mixture to egg mixture, stirring with a wooden spoon to mix well. Stir in nuts. Pour batter into prepared pan. Bake for about 20 minutes or until top springs back when touched lightly with finger. Cool in pan on a wire rack.

While bars are cooling, combine confectioner's sugar, butter, orange juice, and orange peel in a mixer bowl and mix until smooth. Spread over cooled date bars in pan; cut into bars. Makes 24.

LION HOUSE

Cherry Almond Squares

1 package white cake mix
¼ cup all-purpose flour
¼ cup water
2 eggs
¾ cup sour cream
1 can cherry pie filling
Sliced almonds, toasted

Almond Glaze
2 cups powdered sugar
1 teaspoon almond extract
¼ cup half-and-half or
  evaporated milk

PREHEAT OVEN TO 350° F. Combine cake mix and flour in a large bowl. In a separate bowl, whisk together water and eggs. Add to flour mixture along with sour cream. Fold all ingredients together by hand. Spread batter in greased and floured half-sheet pan. Drop small spoonfuls of cherry pie filling over the top. Bake for 20 to 25 minutes. Drizzle with Almond Glaze and sprinkle with sliced almonds. Serves 15 to 20.

IN A SMALL MIXER BOWL MIX all ingredients together until creamy. Drizzle over Cherry Almond Squares.

LION HOUSE

Raisin Squares

1 cup raisins (seeded raisins are best)
1½ cups water
2 tablespoons margarine
2 cups flour
1 cup sugar
1 teaspoon baking powder
1 teaspoon baking soda
1 teaspoon salt
1 teaspoon cinnamon
½ teaspoon nutmeg
1 cup chopped nuts (optional)

Lemon Glaze
1½ cups confectioner's sugar
2 tablespoons skim milk
1 teaspoon finely shredded lemon peel
2 teaspoons lemon juice

PREHEAT OVEN TO 350° F. Spray a 13x9-inch baking pan with nonstick cooking spray; set aside.

Combine raisins and water in a medium saucepan. Boil uncovered until 1 cup of liquid remains. Add margarine to raisin mixture; stir until melted. In a large bowl, combine flour, sugar, baking powder, baking soda, salt, cinnamon, nutmeg, and nuts. Add raisin mixture and mix until well combined. Spread in prepared pan and bake for 18 to 20 minutes or until golden brown. Spread with Lemon Glaze, if desired. Cut into squares. Makes 30.

IN A SMALL BOWL STIR TOGETHER sugar, milk, lemon peel, and lemon juice until smooth and of drizzling consistency.

LION HOUSE

Butter Pecan Squares

½ cup butter, softened
½ cup packed brown sugar
1 egg
1 teaspoon vanilla
¾ cup flour
2 cups milk chocolate chips
¾ cup chopped pecans

IN A LARGE MIXER BOWL CREAM butter, sugar, egg, and vanilla till light and fluffy. Blend in flour. Stir in 1 cup chocolate chips and ½ cup pecans. Pour into greased 8-inch square baking dish. Bake at 350° F. for 25 to 30 minutes. Remove from oven and immediately sprinkle with remaining 1 cup chips. When chips melt, spread evenly over top with knife. Sprinkle with ¼ cup pecans. Cool, then cut into squares. Makes 16.

LION HOUSE

Oatmeal Fudge Bars

1 cup margarine

2 cups brown sugar

2 eggs

2 teaspoons vanilla

2½ cups flour

1 teaspoon baking soda

½ teaspoon salt

1½ cups quick-cooking oats

1 14-ounce can sweetened
  condensed milk

1 12-ounce package semi-
  sweet chocolate chips

¼ cup margarine

2 teaspoons vanilla

1 cup chopped walnuts
  (optional)

PREHEAT OVEN TO 350° F. GREASE a 9x13x2-inch baking pan. Set aside. In a large mixer bowl cream margarine and brown sugar; add eggs and vanilla. In a small bowl sift flour, baking soda, and salt; add to creamed mixture. Mix in oats. In heavy saucepan mix sweetened condensed milk, chocolate chips, and margarine and heat till just melted. Stir in vanilla and nuts.

Spread two-thirds of the dough into prepared baking pan. Spread with chocolate mixture. Drop remaining one-third of dough on top by spoonfuls. Bake for 25 minutes. Cool, then cut into bars. Makes 36.

LION HOUSE

Baked Fudge

4 ounces baking chocolate

½ cup milk

4 eggs

2 cups sugar

1 teaspoon salt

1 cup all-purpose flour,
  sifted

2 teaspoons vanilla

2 cups nuts, chopped

⅔ cup melted butter

Whipping cream (optional)

PREHEAT OVEN TO 350° F. GREASE and flour a 9x13x2-inch pan. Cut chocolate into small pieces and place in a small saucepan with milk. Stir and cook over a low heat until mixture forms a smooth, thick paste. Set aside to cool. In a large mixing bowl, beat the eggs. Stir in sugar until it dissolves into the eggs. Add cooled chocolate paste into the egg mixture. In a separate bowl add salt to sifted flour and sift again into egg mixture. Stir in vanilla and chopped nuts. Fold melted butter in with other ingredients. Beat well and turn into prepared pan. Bake for 40 to 45 minutes. Allow to cool and cut into 3-inch squares. Serve with whipped cream, if desired.

Note: May be served by placing a cloud of whipped cream in a small bowl and putting fudge in the middle of cream. Fudge can be scooped instead of cut.

LION HOUSE

Brownies

1 cup plus 5 tablespoons
    margarine
1 cup cocoa
2⅔ cups sugar
6 large eggs
2⅔ cups all-purpose flour
1 cup walnuts, chopped
1 cup chocolate chips
    (optional)

PREHEAT OVEN TO 350° F. GREASE or spray a 9x13x2-inch cake pan. In a large saucepan, melt margarine and cocoa over a low heat. Pour into a large mixing bowl with the sugar and mix until creamy. Add eggs and mix well together, then add flour. Stir in nuts and chocolate chips, if desired. Pour into prepared pan. Bake for 20 to 30 minutes. Cut into 15 to 18 squares.

CARRIAGE COURT

Pecan Brownies

¾ cup butter
¾ cup shortening
3¾ cups sugar
1½ cups cocoa
½ teaspoon salt
⅔ cup corn syrup
½ teaspoon vanilla
4 large eggs
1¾ cups all-purpose flour
¾ cup pecans

PREHEAT OVEN TO 325° F. GREASE or spray a 9x13x2-inch cake pan. Set aside. In a large mixing bowl, cream butter, shortening, and sugar. Add cocoa, salt, corn syrup, and vanilla and beat until evenly blended. Add eggs and continue mixing until blended. Add flour and mix until just blended. Fold in pecans. Pour into prepared pan. Bake for 45 to 50 minutes. Cut into 15 to 18 squares.

LION HOUSE

Pecan Bars

Topping

1½ cups butter
1½ cups brown sugar
1½ cups honey
½ cup heavy whipping cream
4 cups pecans

MAKE THE TOPPING FIRST AND allow it to cool while preparing and baking the crust. To make the topping, mix butter, sugar, and honey in a saucepan over medium heat. Bring to a boil and cook until it has boiled 5 minutes, stirring constantly. Remove from heat. Cool slightly and add cream and pecans.

Crust

1 cup butter
1 cup sugar
3 eggs
Grated rind of 1 lemon
4 cups all-purpose flour
½ teaspoon baking powder

TO MAKE CRUST: Preheat oven to 375° F. Grease a sheet cake pan. In a large mixing bowl, cream butter and sugar. Add eggs and lemon rind; beat until smooth. Add flour and baking powder and mix well. Press the dough into the bottom of the pan, pricking evenly with a fork. Bake 12 to 15 minutes or until dough looks half done. (Overbaking at this point will cause the crust to be too hard by the time the second baking is complete.) Reduce heat to 350° F. Spread topping evenly over the partially baked crust and bake for an additional 30 to 35 minutes or until topping is set. Cut into bars. Makes about 15 to 24 bars, depending on size.

LION HOUSE

Pictured on page 125.

Cream Cheese Brownies

1 package deluxe brownie
    mix
8 ounces cream cheese,
    softened
⅓ cup sugar
1 egg
2 tablespoons milk

FOLLOW PACKAGE DIRECTIONS FOR cake-like brownies; place in a 9x9-inch pan. In a separate bowl, combine cream cheese and sugar until creamy. Add eggs and milk; mix until smooth. Drop cream cheese batter into the brownie pan in spoonfuls and swirl. Bake for 35 to 40 minutes. Cut into 3-inch squares or size desired.

Variation: For Raspberry Cream Cheese Brownies, add approximately ½ cup raspberry jam on top of cream cheese before swirling.

LION HOUSE

Pictured on page 125.

PECAN BARS. RECIPE ON PAGE 124.
CREAM CHEESE BROWNIES. RECIPE ON PAGE 124.
LEMON BARS. RECIPE ON PAGE 126.

Lemon Bars

1¼ cups butter
2¼ cups all-purpose flour
½ cup powdered sugar

To MAKE CRUST: Preheat oven to 350° F. Put butter in mixer bowl and beat until softened. Add flour and powdered sugar and mix on low speed until just combined. Spread dough evenly in a 9x13-inch pan. Bake for 10 minutes or until the corners are light golden brown. Remove from oven and pour filling on top of crust.

Filling

4 eggs
2 cups sugar
6 tablespoons lemon juice
4 tablespoons all-purpose
   flour
1 teaspoon baking powder

To MAKE FILLING: In a small mixing bowl, mix together eggs, sugar, lemon juice, flour, and baking powder with a wire whisk or on low speed of a mixer for just a few minutes. (It is important not to mix a lot of air into the filling.) Pour on top of partially baked crust and bake for 30 to 35 minutes. Allow to cool slightly and dust with powdered sugar. Cut into small bars. Makes 18 to 24.

LION HOUSE

Pictured on page 125.

Lemon Squares

½ cup butter or margarine,
   softened
¼ cup plus a few tablespoons
   powdered sugar
1 cup flour

PREHEAT OVEN TO 325° F. In a large bowl, cream butter and ¼ cup powdered sugar; add 1 cup flour. Spread in an 8x8-inch pan and bake for 15 to 20 minutes. While crust is baking, prepare filling.

Filling

2 eggs
1 cup sugar
2 tablespoons flour
2 tablespoons lemon juice
Grated rind of ½ lemon

IN A MEDIUM BOWL, beat eggs slightly and add sugar, 2 tablespoons flour, lemon juice, and lemon rind. Mix well and pour over hot crust immediately after removing it from the oven. Bake for 15 to 20 minutes. Remove from oven and sprinkle with sifted powdered sugar. Cool slightly before cutting into 2-inch squares. Serve with vanilla ice cream, if desired. Makes 16.

LION HOUSE

Chocolate-Dipped Orange Cookies

2 cups flour
½ cup yellow cornmeal
1 teaspoon salt
½ teaspoon baking soda
1 cup butter, softened
1 cup sugar
2 egg yolks
1 tablespoon grated orange
    peel
1 teaspoon orange extract
¼ cup ground walnuts
6 ounces milk chocolate or
    semisweet chocolate
    chips

IN A BOWL, STIR TOGETHER FLOUR, cornmeal, salt, and baking soda. Set aside. In a large bowl, cream together butter and sugar. Beat in egg yolks, orange peel, and orange extract until fluffy. Add flour mixture and walnuts. Mix well. Divide dough in half. Wrap in plastic and refrigerate for 30 minutes.

Preheat oven to 350° F. Roll half of the dough out to ¼-inch thickness on a lightly floured surface. Cut dough with a floured 3½-inch round or star-shaped cookie cutter. If using round cutter, cut each circle in half. Place 1 inch apart on a lightly greased baking sheet. Repeat with remaining dough. Bake in preheated oven for 10 to 12 minutes or until lightly browned. Cool on a wire rack.

Line a baking sheet with wax paper. In a small saucepan, melt chocolate over low heat, stirring constantly. (Or chocolate may be melted in microwave in a microwave-safe bowl.) Remove from heat. Dip one end of each cookie into chocolate; place on prepared sheet. Let stand until chocolate hardens, about 1 hour. Makes 30.

LION HOUSE

Chocolate Orange Logs

1 cup butter or margarine
½ cup sifted powdered sugar
1 teaspoon grated orange
    rind
1 teaspoon orange flavoring
2 cups flour
1 cup chocolate chips
½ cup finely chopped nuts

PREHEAT OVEN TO 350° F. IN A large mixing bowl cream butter; gradually add sugar, beating till light and fluffy. Stir in orange rind and orange flavoring. Gradually add flour. Shape dough into a long roll ¾-inch wide. Cut roll into 2-inch pieces. Place on greased cookie sheet. Flatten one end of each piece lengthwise with fork. Bake at 350° F. for 10 minutes, or till light brown. Cool cookies on wire rack. Melt chocolate chips in microwave oven or in top of double boiler over simmering water. Dip unflattened ends of cookies in chocolate; then roll in chopped nuts. Store in covered container. Makes 4 dozen cookies.

LION HOUSE

Almond Cookies

1 cup sugar

1 cup butter

2 eggs

2 tablespoons water

1½ tablespoons almond
    flavoring

3½ cups all-purpose flour

1½ teaspoons salt

1½ teaspoons soda

1 cup almonds, sliced and
    toasted

PREHEAT OVEN TO 350° F. In a large mixing bowl combine butter and sugar until light and fluffy. Add eggs, water, and almond flavoring and beat well. Add flour, salt, and soda and mix until well combined. Add almonds and mix well. On a floured board using a floured rolling pin, roll out dough to a ¼-inch thickness and cut out in desired shapes. Bake on a greased cookie sheet for 10 minutes or until edges are slightly brown. Makes 3 to 4 dozen cookies.

LION HOUSE

Sunflower Seed Cookies

1 cup butter

1 cup granulated sugar

¾ cup brown sugar

¼ cup honey

2 eggs

1 teaspoon vanilla

2¾ cups flour

1 teaspoon soda

½ teaspoon baking powder

2 cups oatmeal

½ teaspoon salt*

⅔ cup sunflower seeds,
    shelled

1 cup coconut

PREHEAT OVEN TO 350° F. In a large mixing bowl, blend butter and sugars until light and fluffy. Add honey, eggs, and vanilla; beat at medium speed until light and fluffy. Add flour, soda, baking powder, oatmeal, and salt. When ingredients are well incorporated, turn off the mixer and scrape down the sides of the bowl. Add sunflower seeds and coconut. Mix again briefly, then drop by rounded tablespoonfuls onto a greased cookie sheet. Bake for 8 to 10 minutes. Makes 3 to 4 dozen cookies.

*If using salted sunflower seeds, decrease salt to ¼ teaspoon.

LION HOUSE

Granola Bars

1 14-ounce package choco-
  late caramels
2 tablespoons water
¾ cup crunchy peanut
  butter
3 cups plain granola
1 cup golden raisins
½ cup salted peanuts

MELT CARAMELS IN WATER over medium heat in heavy saucepan, stirring often. Stir in peanut butter. Add granola, raisins, and peanuts; mix well. Pour into a buttered 9x13-inch pan, and cool. Cut into 1x2-inch bars. Makes about 32 bars.

Variation: Substitute chocolate caramels for plain caramels.

LION HOUSE

Spritz Cookies

½ cup butter, softened
⅓ cup sugar
¼ teaspoon vanilla or
  almond extract
1 egg yolk
1¼ cups flour
Maraschino cherry halves, if
  desired

PREHEAT OVEN TO 375° F. IN A large mixer bowl cream together butter and sugar. Add flavoring and egg yolk. Mix in flour gradually. Put dough into cookie press and force into desired shapes onto an ungreased baking sheet. Decorate each cookie with a maraschino cherry half, if desired. Bake at 375° F. for 7 to 10 minutes. Remove cookies immediately from baking pan to wire racks. Makes 2 dozen cookies.

LION HOUSE

Crescent Cookies

1 cup butter
2 egg yolks
2 cups powdered sugar
2¼ cups flour
1 teaspoon cinnamon
½ teaspoon cloves
⅛ teaspoon salt
2 cups ground, blanched
    almonds
Powdered sugar

PREHEAT OVEN TO 350° F. GREASE a cookie sheet and set aside. Beat butter and egg yolks together in a large bowl. Add powdered sugar and beat until well mixed. Add flour, cinnamon, cloves, salt, and ground almonds. Mix well. Pinch off a piece of dough about the size of a walnut; roll it into a 2-inch rope and form it into a crescent shape. Place on prepared cookie sheet. Repeat with remaining dough. Bake for 20 minutes. While cookies are still warm, roll them in powdered sugar. Makes 2 dozen.

LION HOUSE

Wedding Cookies

½ cup sugar
1 cup butter
1 teaspoon vanilla
2 cups all-purpose flour
1 cup walnuts or pecans,
    chopped
Powdered sugar

PREHEAT OVEN TO 350° F. Line a cookie sheet with wax paper. Set aside. In a large mixing bowl, cream sugar, butter, and vanilla together. Add flour and mix well. Add nuts and mix. Roll into 1½-inch balls and place on prepared cookie sheet. Bake for 10 to 12 minutes. (The tops of cookies should have slight cracks in them and the bottom edges should be just barely light golden brown.) Roll cookies in powdered sugar while very warm. Makes 3 dozen cookies.

LION HOUSE

Coconut-Cherry Macaroons

1 7-ounce bag sweetened, shredded coconut, coarsely chopped
½ cup canned soft almond paste
½ cup chopped red candied cherries
½ cup chopped green candied cherries
¼ cup sugar
¼ cup flour
¼ teaspoon salt
2 egg whites, lightly beaten

PREHEAT OVEN TO 325° F. Line a baking sheet with wax paper; set aside. In a large bowl, combine coconut, almond paste, candied cherries, sugar, flour, salt, and egg whites. Stir until well mixed. Drop mixture by level tablespoonfuls onto prepared baking sheet, shaping into rounds. Bake in preheated oven for 25 minutes, until lightly browned but still soft in the center. Cool on wire rack. Makes 2 dozen.

LION HOUSE

Million-Dollar Cookies

2 cups shortening
1 cup granulated sugar
1 cup brown sugar
2 eggs
1 teaspoon vanilla
1 teaspoon almond flavoring
4 cups flour
2 teaspoons baking soda
2 teaspoons cream of tartar

GREASE A COOKIE SHEET and set aside. In a large mixer bowl cream shortening, sugars, eggs, vanilla, and almond flavoring till fluffy. In another bowl sift flour, baking soda, and cream of tartar together. Add gradually to creamed mixture. Chill. Mold dough into 1-inch balls. Place onto prepared cookie sheet. Flatten each cookie with bottom of a drinking glass dipped in sugar. Bake for 10 minutes at 350° F. Cool on wire rack. Store in covered container. Makes 5 dozen cookies.

Variations: Add chocolate chips, chopped nuts, or raisins to batter before chilling. Drop by spoonfuls onto cookie sheet and bake as above.

LION HOUSE

CRANBERRY NUT BREAD. RECIPE ON PAGE 140.

Banana Bread

6 large or 8 medium
    bananas, very ripe
4 eggs
2 cups sugar
¾ cup oil
4 cups flour
1 teaspoon soda
2 teaspoons salt
2 teaspoons baking powder
½ cup walnuts, chopped

PREHEAT OVEN TO 325° F. Prepare 2 large loaf pans by greasing and flouring well. Set aside. Peel bananas and place in a large mixing bowl; mix until bananas are mashed. Add eggs, sugar, and oil to the bananas and mix until well blended. In a separate bowl, mix flour, soda, salt, and baking powder. Add this mixture to the banana mixture. Mix together until the ingredients are blended. Add the nuts and mix briefly. (Overmixing causes tunnels and a coarse texture.)

Pour into prepared pans. Bake for 50 to 60 minutes or until wooden toothpick inserted in center comes out clean. Makes 2 loaves.

Note: You can make smaller loaves if desired. Adjust baking time according to size; the smaller the loaf the shorter the baking time.

LION HOUSE

Applesauce Fruit Loaf

1 cup flour
¾ pound candied fruit
    mixture
½ cup chopped dates
¼ cup butter
½ cup sugar
1 teaspoon baking soda
¾ cup applesauce
¼ teaspoon cloves
½ teaspoon cinnamon
¼ teaspoon salt
1 egg, beaten
1 cup seedless raisins
½ cup chopped nut meats

PREHEAT OVEN TO 300° F. Grease well a 8x4-inch loaf pan. Set aside. In a large bowl add flour to candied fruit and dates. In a large mixer bowl cream butter and sugar together. In a small bowl add soda to applesauce; combine with butter and sugar mixture, then add spices, salt, and egg. Combine this mixture with the fruit-flour mixture. Stir in raisins and nuts. Pour into prepared pan and bake for 1 hour or until wooden toothpick inserted in center comes out clean. Makes 1 loaf.

LION HOUSE

Chocolate-Banana Almond Bread

2 or 3 medium ripe bananas
    (1 cup mashed)
1½ cups flour
1 cup sugar
6 tablespoons unsweetened
    cocoa
1 teaspoon baking soda
½ teaspoon salt
¼ teaspoon baking powder
2 eggs
⅓ cup vegetable oil
⅓ cup chopped almonds

PREHEAT OVEN TO 350° F. Spray a 9x5-inch loaf pan with non-stick cooking spray; set aside. Mash bananas with fork and measure to make 1 cup. In a large bowl, mix together flour, sugar, cocoa, baking soda, salt, and baking powder. Make a well in the center of the dry ingredients. In a separate bowl, beat eggs, oil, and mashed bananas. Pour into well in dry mixture; mix until just moistened. Stir in almonds. Pour into prepared loaf pan. Bake for 55 to 60 minutes, or until wooden toothpick inserted in center comes out clean. Let stand in pan for 10 minutes, then turn out onto wire rack to cool. Makes 1 loaf, about 16 slices.

LION HOUSE

Janell's Poppy Seed Bread

¼ cup butter, melted
3⅓ tablespoons oil
2 eggs
½ cup milk
¾ cup sugar
½ teaspoon vanilla
½ teaspoon almond extract
1 cup all-purpose flour
½ teaspoon salt
1 teaspoon baking powder
¾ teaspoon poppy seeds

PREHEAT OVEN TO 325° F. Grease and flour an 8x4-inch loaf pan and set aside. In a large mixing bowl cream together butter, oil, eggs, milk, sugar, vanilla, and almond extract. In a separate bowl mix together flour, salt, baking powder, and poppy seeds. Add this mixture to the first and mix until well blended, but do not overmix. (Overmixing causes tunnels and a coarse texture.)

Pour into loaf pan and bake for 45 minutes. Serve plain or, while bread is still hot, brush with several coats of Orange Almond Glaze. Makes 1 loaf.

Orange Almond Glaze
1 tablespoon orange juice
¼ teaspoon vanilla
¼ teaspoon almond extract
¼ cup powdered sugar

IN A SMALL BOWL MIX ALL ingredients together to make icing.

LION HOUSE

Date Nut Bread

1¼ cups flour
1⅓ teaspoons soda
¾ teaspoon salt
⅔ cup dates, chopped
⅔ cup boiling water
⅔ cup brown sugar, lightly
    packed
2½ tablespoons oil
2 eggs
⅓ cup nuts, chopped

PREHEAT OVEN TO 325° F. Line a 8x4-inch bread pan with wax paper and set aside. In a medium bowl, mix together flour, soda, and salt. Set aside. Place chopped dates in a small bowl. Pour the boiling water over the dates and then allow to cool until lukewarm. While dates are cooling, cream together brown sugar, oil, and eggs in a large mixing bowl. Blend in date mixture. Add flour mixture, then add chopped nuts. Mix well.

Pour into bread pan and bake for 35 to 40 minutes. Makes 1 loaf, 10 to 12 slices.

LION HOUSE

Zucchini Bread

3 cups all-purpose flour
1 teaspoon soda
½ teaspoon baking powder
2 teaspoons cinnamon
3 eggs
1 cup oil
2 cups sugar
1 tablespoon vanilla
2 cups zucchini, grated
1 cup walnuts, chopped

PREHEAT OVEN TO 325° F. Grease well 1 large 8x4-inch loaf pan or 2 small 7x3-inch loaf pans. Set aside. In a large bowl mix together flour, soda, baking powder, and cinnamon. Set aside. In a separate mixing bowl beat eggs until light and foamy. Add oil, sugar, vanilla, and zucchini; mix well. Add the flour mixture and mix just until moist. (Overmixing causes tunnels and a coarse texture.) Fold in nuts.

Pour into prepared pan or pans. Pans should be about two-thirds full. Bake for 45 to 50 minutes for large loaf or 35 minutes for small loaves or until a wooden toothpick inserted in center comes out clean. Do not overbake. Serves 10 to 12.

LION HOUSE

Lion House Pumpkin Bread

1⅓ cups vegetable oil

5 eggs

1 16-ounce can pumpkin

2 cups flour

2 cups sugar

1 teaspoon salt

1 teaspoon cinnamon

1 teaspoon nutmeg

1 teaspoon baking soda

2 3-ounce packages vanilla
    pudding mix (instant)

1 cup chopped nuts

PREHEAT OVEN TO 350° F. Grease well 2 large 8x4-inch loaf pans. Set aside. Mix oil, eggs, and pumpkin in mixing bowl and beat well. In another bowl sift together flour, sugar, salt, cinnamon, nutmeg, and baking soda. Add to pumpkin mixture and mix till blended. Stir in pudding mix and nuts. Pour into prepared loaf pans. Bake for 1 hour. Makes 2 loaves.

LION HOUSE

Aloha Bread

1 cup butter

2 cups sugar

4 eggs

1 cup mashed bananas

4 cups all-purpose flour

2 teaspoons baking powder

1 teaspoon soda

¾ teaspoon salt

1 20-ounce can crushed
    pineapple, undrained

¾ cup chopped pecans

1 cup coconut

PREHEAT OVEN TO 325° F. Grease 2 large 8x4-inch loaf pans. Set aside. In a large mixing bowl cream butter and sugar. Add eggs. Stir in bananas. In a separate bowl mix flour, baking powder, soda, and salt, then add to banana mixture. Blend well, but be careful not to overmix. (Overmixing causes tunnels and a coarse texture.) Add pineapple, pecans, and coconut and mix together on low speed until blended. Pour into prepared pans. The pans should each be two-thirds full. Bake for 60 to 80 minutes. Makes 2 large loaves.

LION HOUSE

Pictured on page 139.

ALOHA BREAD. RECIPE ON PAGE 138.

Cherry Nut Bread

1 cup sugar

½ cup oil

2 eggs

1 teaspoon vanilla

2¼ cups all-purpose flour

1 teaspoon baking powder

½ cup maraschino cherry
    juice

1 8-ounce jar maraschino
    cherries, slightly
    chopped

½ cup walnuts, chopped

Powdered sugar

PREHEAT OVEN TO 325° F. Grease and flour two 8x4-inch bread pans or line with wax paper. Set aside. In a large mixing bowl cream sugar and oil; add eggs and beat well. Stir in vanilla. In a separate bowl mix together flour and baking powder. Pour maraschino cherry juice from 8-ounce jar into a ½ cup measure. If there isn't enough juice to equal ½ cup, add water to make up the rest. Alternately add flour mixture and maraschino cherry juice to first mixture until all is blended together. Stir in cherries and nuts.

Pour into bread pans and bake for 55 to 60 minutes or until wooden toothpick inserted in center comes out clean. Sprinkle powdered sugar on top of warm loaf. Store wrapped in plastic. Makes 2 loaves.

Note: Bread is good immediately, but is better after a day or two.

LION HOUSE

Cranberry Nut Bread

2 cups all-purpose flour

1 teaspoon baking powder

½ teaspoon soda

1 teaspoon salt

⅓ cup butter

¾ cup sugar

2 eggs

¾ cup orange juice

1 tablespoon grated orange
    peel

1 cup fresh cranberries
    (chopped, if desired)

½ cup chopped nuts

PREHEAT OVEN TO 350° F. Grease and flour one large 8x4-inch loaf pan or two small 7x3-inch loaf pans. Set aside. In a medium bowl mix flour, baking powder, soda, and salt. In a mixer bowl, cream butter until soft and add sugar. Beat until creamy, then add eggs, orange juice, and orange peel. Beat until well mixed. Scrape down the sides and bottom of the bowl and add the dry ingredients. Mix until incorporated, but do not overmix. (The mixer should not be turned on higher than low while mixing the dry ingredients in.) Stir in the cranberries and nuts by hand. Pour batter into prepared loaf pan or pans. Bake 45 to 50 minutes at 350° F. for the large loaf and less time for the small loaves. Cool completely before slicing. Makes 1 large or 2 small loaves.

LION HOUSE

Pictured on page 132.

Orange Nut Bread

1 medium orange
1 cup raisins or dates
2 tablespoons melted butter
   or margarine
1 teaspoon vanilla
1 egg, beaten
2 cups flour
½ teaspoon salt
1 teaspoon baking powder
½ teaspoon baking soda
1 cup sugar
1 cup chopped nuts

PREHEAT OVEN TO 350° F. GREASE well a 8x4-inch loaf pan. Set aside. Wash orange; squeeze juice. Pour juice into a one-cup measure; if there isn't enough juice to equal a full cup, add boiling water to make up the rest. Put orange rind and raisins through a chopper. (Raisins may be left whole if desired.) Combine butter, vanilla, and egg; pour onto chopped fruits. Sift dry ingredients together in a bowl and add to fruit mixture. Stir in nuts last. Pour into prepared pan. Bake 1 hour. Makes 1 loaf.

Note: If orange has a thick skin, remove as much of the white part under the skin as possible before grinding.

LION HOUSE

Baklava

1 pound walnuts
1 pound almonds
1 tablespoon cinnamon
1 pound filo dough sheets
1½ to 2 cups melted butter
Whole cloves (optional)

To MAKE PASTRY: Grind walnuts and almonds in a meat grinder or blender. Mix in cinnamon. Set aside. Place filo dough in a bowl and cover bowl with damp cloth, making sure cloth does not touch dough. Butter a 13x9-inch pan. Place 3 filo sheets on bottom of pan. Spread liberally with melted butter. Sprinkle with some of the ground nuts and cinnamon mixture. Repeat layers, using 2 sheets of filo each time instead of 3, until pan is nearly filled. End with 3 sheets of filo. Cut into diamonds with sharp knife. Place whole clove in the middle of each diamond, if desired. Bake at 300° F. for 55 to 60 minutes. If pastry gets too brown, cover with foil for the last few minutes of baking time.

Syrup

4 cups sugar
2 cups water
1 cup honey
1 cinnamon stick
1 slice fresh lemon

To MAKE SYRUP: In a medium saucepan, combine sugar, water, honey, cinnamon stick, and lemon slice. Boil gently, stirring occasionally, for 10 to 15 minutes. Remove from heat, discard cinnamon stick and lemon slice, and let syrup cool.

Directly after removing baklava from oven, pour half of the cooled syrup evenly over the top. Wait one hour and then pour the remaining syrup over the top. Serves 18.

LION HOUSE

Kringle

4 cups flour
3 tablespoons sugar
¾ teaspoon salt
1 cup butter
2 packages active dry yeast
¼ cup lukewarm water
1 cup milk
3 eggs, beaten
1 teaspoon cardamom
1 egg white, slightly beaten
Sugar
Cinnamon
Slivered almonds

IN A LARGE BOWL, COMBINE FLOUR, sugar, and salt. Cut in butter with a pastry blender. In a small bowl dissolve yeast in warm water and set aside. In a small saucepan scald milk, allow to cool slightly, and add gradually to beaten eggs in a large bowl. Add the dissolved yeast, cardamon, and flour mixture. Mix until smooth. Cover and let rise until double (1 to 1½ hours).

Turn dough out onto a floured board and knead gently 2 or 3 times. Divide dough in half and place on 2 large, well-greased baking sheets. Spread dough into a thin rectangle on each sheet. Spread Almond Filling down the middle of one rectangle of dough and Raisin Filling down the middle of the other. Fold 2 long edges in to meet in the center and press together to seal. Brush egg white over tops of loaves; sprinkle with sugar, cinnamon, and slivered almonds. Bake at 350° F. for 30 minutes or until lightly browned. Serves 20.

Almond Filling

2 tablespoons butter,
    softened
¼ cup sugar
1 egg yolk
½ teaspoon rum flavoring
½ cup ground almonds

IN A SMALL MIXING BOWL, BEAT BUTTER until creamy. Add sugar slowly and beat until fluffy. Beat in egg yolk and rum flavoring. Fold in almonds.

Raisin Filling

1 cup seedless raisins
1¼ cups water
¼ cup sugar
½ teaspoon grated lemon
    peel
¼ cup ground almonds

GRIND RAISINS IN A FOOD CHOPPER. Place in small saucepan with water, sugar, and lemon peel. Cook over medium heat, stirring constantly, until thick and smooth (about 5 minutes). Cool. Fold in almonds.

LION HOUSE

Danish Pastry

1 cup softened butter or
    margarine
2 cups warm milk
2 tablespoons yeast
1 tablespoon sugar
½ cup warm water
¾ cup sugar
1 teaspoon salt
2 eggs
8 cups flour
Sliced or slivered almonds

PLACE ALL INGREDIENTS EXCEPT almonds in a large mixing bowl. Mix till well blended but do not overmix. Cover and let rise till double. Punch down. In the meantime, make Cream Filling, Almond Filling, Steusel Topping, and Almond Icing.

DIRECTIONS FOR ASSEMBLING: Divide dough into 4 equal parts. On lightly floured board, roll out each part into a rectangle. Spread one-fourth Cream Filling on each; then one-fourth Almond Filling on each. Roll up jelly-roll fashion. Cut about 10 slashes through top with knife. Place each roll on greased cookie sheet. Sprinkle with Streusel Topping. Let rise in a warm place till double in bulk. Bake at 375° F. for 20 minutes. Drizzle with Almond Icing and sprinkle with sliced or slivered almonds.

Cream Filling
1 cup milk
1 egg yolk
½ teaspoon salt
⅓ cup sugar
2 tablespoons flour

HEAT MILK IN SAUCEPAN. Mix egg yolk into dry ingredients. Add a little warm milk, then mix with heated milk and stir and cook till thick. Cover with plastic wrap and cool.

Almond Filling
½ cup butter or margarine
¾ cup sugar
½ cup oats
2 teaspoons almond flavor-
    ing

MIX ALL INGREDIENTS WITH fork or wire whip or mixer till well blended.

Streusel Topping
½ cup flour
½ cup sugar
½ cup butter

MIX ALL INGREDIENTS with fork or wire whip or mixer till well blended.

Almond Icing
1 cup powdered sugar
2 to 3 tablespoons milk or
    cream
1 teaspoon almond flavoring

COMBINE POWDERED SUGAR with enough milk or cream to make slightly runny icing. Add almond flavoring.

LION HOUSE

Lion House Fruit Cake

½ cup plus 1 tablespoon
    butter
1 cup sugar
3½ cups all-purpose flour
1 tablespoon soda
Dash ground cloves
Dash cinnamon
¾ teaspoon salt
1¾ cups applesauce
2 eggs
⅛ teaspoon imitation rum
    flavoring
¼ teaspoon vanilla
4½ cups fruit mix
    (1¾ pounds)
2 cups dates, cut up
2 cups raisins
1 cup pecans, chopped

IN A LARGE BOWL, CREAM together butter and sugar with an electric mixer for 2 minutes on low speed. In a separate bowl, sift together flour, soda, ground cloves, cinnamon, and salt. Add this to the creamed mixture and mix on low speed for about 5 minutes. The mixture will be very dry. Add applesauce, eggs, rum flavoring, and vanilla. Mix until blended. Then add fruit mix, dates, raisins, and pecans to the batter and mix in by hand.

Line loaf pans with wax paper. Divide batter evenly between pans.

FOR LARGE LOAVES: Bake in a slow oven (200° F.) for 1¼ hours. Then gradually bring the temperature up to 325° F., allowing fruit cake to bake about 5 minutes between each temperature adjustment. Cake will need to bake 30 to 40 minutes more from the time temperature adjustment starts.

FOR SMALL LOAVES: Bake in a slow oven (200° F.) for 1 hour. Then gradually bring the temperature to 325° F. during the next 20 to 30 minutes.

Cake is done when wooden toothpick inserted in center comes out clean. Remove from oven and while still hot, brush cakes with two or three coats of Syrup Icing.

Syrup Icing

½ cup water
1 cup light corn syrup
⅛ teaspoon imitation rum
    flavoring

STIR TOGETHER WATER, CORN SYRUP, and rum flavoring together to make icing. Ice cakes while still hot.

After cakes have cooled, remove wax paper and wrap in plastic wrap. Put in a cool place and let mellow for about 2 weeks before cutting. The longer fruit cake mellows, the better it is. Makes 2 large loaves or 4 small loaves.

LION HOUSE

Sweet Breads

Al's Holiday Raisin Fruit Cake

4½ cups seedless raisins

2 tablespoons lemon juice

⅓ cup orange rind, grated

⅔ cup grape juice

1⅓ cups butter

1 cup plus 2 tablespoons
brown sugar

5 eggs

2 tablespoons molasses

2¾ cups all-purpose flour

1 teaspoon baking powder

1⅓ teaspoons cinnamon

½ teaspoon ground cloves

1 teaspoon allspice

1 cup chopped nuts
(optional)

IN A MIXING BOWL COMBINE RAISINS, lemon juice, orange rind, and grape juice. Cover and allow to stand overnight. In a large mixing bowl, cream butter until soft and smooth. Add brown sugar, beating until light and fluffy. Add eggs a few at a time, beating after each addition until well mixed. Continue beating until light and fluffy. Add molasses and mix well. In a separate bowl, sift flour, baking powder, cinnamon, ground cloves, and allspice together twice. Add gradually to sugar mixture, beating after each addition until well mixed. Add fruit and nuts with last amount of dry ingredients. Mix well, but do not overmix. Divide batter equally in 3 small 7x3-inch loaf pans lined with wax paper. Bake in a slow oven (200° F.) for 1 hour. Increase heat to 250° F. and bake for 15 more minutes, then increase heat to 300° F. and bake for 30 more minutes or until done. Brush with a simple syrup while fruit cake is still hot. After cake has cooled, wrap in plastic wrap. Allow to mellow at least 2 weeks. Makes 3 small loaves.

Syrup

½ cup water

1 cup light corn syrup

⅛ teaspoon imitation rum
flavoring

STIR TOGETHER WATER, corn syrup, and rum flavoring to make syrup.

LION HOUSE

Fruit Cake

2 cups chopped dates

3 cups raisins

1 cup candied pineapple and
    cherries

1 pound fruit cake mix

2 cups pecan halves

2 cups flour

½ teaspoon salt

½ teaspoon cloves

½ teaspoon mace

¼ teaspoon soda

1 teaspoon cinnamon

1 cup melted butter

1¼ cups brown sugar

4 eggs

¼ cup honey

¼ cup fruit juice

IN A MIXING BOWL COMBINE dates, raisins, pineapple and cherries, fruit cake mix, and nuts. Set aside. In a very large bowl mix together flour, salt, cloves, mace, soda, and cinnamon. Add the fruit and nut mixture to the flour mixture. Stir until fruit and nut mixture is evenly coated with flour mixture. Pay special attention to the dates to make sure they are coated.

In a large mixer bowl mix together butter, brown sugar, eggs, honey, and fruit juice. Stir into the flour and fruit mixture. Spoon into loaf pans that have been lined with oiled brown paper (grocery bags). Fill pans three-fourths full. This will make two 8x4-inch loaves or several smaller-sized loaves.

Place fruit cakes on second level of the oven. Put a pan of water on the bottom level. Check the oven periodically during baking to be sure there is still water in the pan; add more water if necessary.

Bake 2½ hours at 275° F. When cool, moisten with additional juice and wrap in foil. Let cakes age at least 2 weeks before eating. Cut with a sharp knife.

LION HOUSE

Doughnut Balls

2½ cups flour

1 teaspoon baking powder

2 eggs

1½ cups sour cream

2 tablespoons sugar

1 teaspoon vanilla

¼ teaspoon salt

1¼ cups vegetable oil for
    deep-frying

1 cup powdered sugar

IN A LARGE MIXING BOWL COMBINE flour, baking powder, eggs, sour cream, sugar, vanilla, and salt until well blended. (The batter will be soft.) Heat oil in a deep skillet until oil is hot enough to fry a 1-inch cube of bread in 1 minute. Carefully place dough by tablespoonfuls into the oil. Fry doughnuts, a few at a time, for 3 to 5 minutes or until golden brown on all sides. Remove from pan with a slotted spoon. Drain on paper towels. When all doughnuts are cooked, pour powdered sugar into a plastic or paper bag. Add a few doughnuts at a time, close bag, and shake gently until doughnuts are well coated. Serve warm. Makes 25.

LION HOUSE

Cinnamon Rolls

2½ cups water
½ cup oil
¾ cup eggs
1 teaspoon vanilla
½ cup milk, powdered
2 tablespoons yeast
1 cup sugar
1 tablespoon salt
7 cups all-purpose flour
Sugar and cinnamon
½ cup butter, melted

PLACE WATER, OIL, EGGS, vanilla, and milk powder in a large mixing bowl and stir vigorously until milk is dissolved. Sprinkle yeast on liquid mixture and add sugar, salt, and flour.

Put in mixer with dough hook and mix for 10 to 15 minutes. The dough will be very sticky. Let rise until double in size. Roll out into rectangle shape. Brush with melted butter. Sprinkle with sugar and cinnamon. Roll up rectangle lengthwise and cut into one-inch slices. Grease a cookie sheet or line with wax paper. Place rolls on cookie sheet and allow to rise until double in size.

Bake at 350° F. for 10 to 12 minutes. After baking, let cool slightly before frosting. Frost with Powdered Sugar Icing or Butter Cream Frosting. Makes 18 rolls.

Note: If you want to make the dough a day ahead, mix dough according to directions. Instead of allowing dough to rise, place it in an oiled bowl, cover with plastic wrap, and refrigerate overnight. When ready to use, remove dough from refrigerator and follow directions for rolling out, rising, and baking. It will take longer for the dough to rise because it will be cold.

Powdered Sugar Icing

2 cups powdered sugar
1 teaspoon vanilla
¼ cup half-and-half or
    evaporated milk

MIX ALL INGREDIENTS TOGETHER in a small mixing bowl and beat until light and well mixed.

Butter Cream Frosting

3 cups powdered sugar
½ cup butter
6 to 8 tablespoons cream or
    evaporated milk
1 teaspoon vanilla

PLACE POWDERED SUGAR IN a mixing bowl. Add butter and 3 tablespoons of the cream. Blend on low speed until mixed. Slowly add the rest of the cream, 1 tablespoon at a time, until creamy and smooth, but not at all runny. Add vanilla and mix again.

LION HOUSE

Frosty Frappé for a Crowd
Recipe on page 160.

Mulled Cranberry Drink

1 12-ounce package fresh
    cranberries
8 cups (2 quarts) water
1½ cups sugar
2 tablespoons grated orange
    peel
6 cinnamon sticks
12 whole cloves
4 cups orange juice
1 cup lemon juice
Thin lemon slices

COMBINE CRANBERRIES, WATER, sugar, orange peel, cinnamon sticks, and cloves in large pan and cook till cranberries are soft, about 15 minutes. Strain. Add juices. Do not boil but keep warm till ready to serve. Float thin lemon slice in each cup. Makes 24 half-cup servings.

LION HOUSE

Lion House Wassail

2¼ cups sugar
4 cups water
2 cinnamon sticks
8 allspice berries
10 cloves
1 piece ginger
4 cups orange juice
2 cups lemon juice
2 quarts apple cider or juice

COMBINE SUGAR AND WATER in a large saucepan. Boil 5 minutes. Remove from heat and add cinnamon sticks, allspice berries, cloves, and ginger. Cover and let stand in warm place for 1 hour. Strain. Just before serving, add juices and cider and bring quickly to boil. Remove from heat and serve. Makes 36 half-cup servings.

LION HOUSE

Holiday Nog

¼ cup sugar

½ teaspoon cinnamon

¼ teaspoon ginger

6 eggs

4 cups orange juice

4 cups pineapple juice

4 cups ginger ale

1 pint orange sherbet

MIX SUGAR, CINNAMON, AND ginger in a large mixer bowl. Add eggs and beat well. Stir in juices. Chill. Just before serving, add ginger ale. Pour into punch bowl and add scoops of sherbet. Makes about 24 half-cup servings.

LION HOUSE

Fiesta Crush

4 cups sugar

6 cups water

5 ripe bananas, peeled and mashed

2½ cups orange juice

4 cups pineapple juice

½ cup lemon juice

2 12-ounce cans carbonated lemon-lime beverage

COMBINE SUGAR AND WATER IN saucepan and heat till sugar is dissolved. Cool. Mash bananas and combine with orange juice, pineapple juice, and lemon juice. Add sugar syrup. Pour into shallow pan and freeze. When ready to serve, remove from freezer to thaw slightly. Break into chunks and fill cups two-thirds full. Pour carbonated lemon-lime beverage over slush. Garnish each serving with a maraschino cherry or sprig of holly, if desired. Makes 25 half-cup servings.

LION HOUSE

Lime Fizz

½ cup fresh lime juice
½ cup sugar
1½ cups pineapple juice
1 quart lime sherbet
1 16-ounce bottle carbon-
    ated lemon-lime
    beverage
Maraschino cherries
Thin slices of lime

PLACE LIME JUICE, SUGAR, AND pineapple juice in blender and whirl for 30 seconds. Add half the lime sherbet and whirl again for a few seconds. Pour into eight 10-ounce glasses (two-thirds full) and fill almost to top with carbonated lemon-lime beverage. Top each cup with a scoop of sherbet. Garnish with maraschino cherry and half slice of fresh lime. Serve with straw. Makes 8 servings.

LION HOUSE

Grape Sparkle

2 cups sugar
4 cups water
2 cups grape juice
2 cups orange juice
½ cup lemon juice
1 12-ounce can carbonated
    ginger ale

COMBINE SUGAR AND WATER IN SAUCEPAN and heat till dissolved. Cool. Add grape juice, orange juice, and lemon juice. Pour into shallow pan and freeze. When ready to serve, remove from freezer and thaw slightly. Break up into chunks and fill punch cups two-thirds full. Pour ginger ale over slush and serve. Makes 20 half-cup servings.

LION HOUSE

Spiced Cranberry Cocktail

4 cups (1 32-ounce bottle)
    cranberry juice cocktail
2 cups orange juice
1 cup unsweetened grape-
    fruit juice
½ cup grenadine syrup
¼ teaspoon ground cloves
¼ teaspoon ground nutmeg

In a large saucepan combine ingredients and heat till warm. Makes 15 half-cup servings.

Lion House

Holly Berry Slush

2 cups sugar
3½ cups water
1 10-ounce package frozen
    raspberries
1 cup orange juice
1 20-ounce can crushed
    pineapple, undrained
¼ cup lemon juice
Red food coloring
    (optional)
2 12-ounce cans carbonated
    lemon-lime beverage

Combine sugar and water in saucepan and heat till sugar is dissolved. Remove from heat and stir in frozen raspberries. Add orange juice, crushed pineapple with juice, lemon juice, and a few drops of red food coloring, if desired. Pour into shallow pan and freeze. Remove from freezer one hour before serving. Break up with fork till slushy. Fill punch cups two-thirds full with slush. Pour carbonated lemon-lime beverage over slush. Makes 20 half-cup servings.

Lion House

Warm Orange Almond Drink

3 cups sugar

4 cups water

1 12-ounce can frozen
    orange juice, undiluted

1½ cups lemon juice

1 tablespoon almond flavor-
    ing

2 teaspoons vanilla

¼ teaspoon ground cloves

¼ teaspoon allspice

¼ teaspoon cinnamon
    (optional)

4 quarts water

HEAT SUGAR AND 4 CUPS WATER IN a pan large enough to hold 6 quarts. Add remaining ingredients and heat till hot. Do not boil. Serve warm. Leftover beverage can be cooled and stored in refrigerator for 10 days. Makes 48 half-cup servings.

LION HOUSE

Lime Slush Punch

2 cups sugar

8 cups water

1 12-ounce can frozen
    limeade

5 fresh limes, juiced

2 12-ounce cans lemon-lime
    carbonated beverage

COMBINE SUGAR AND WATER IN A large saucepan and heat slightly till sugar is dissolved. Add frozen limeade and juice of 5 limes. Mix and pour into shallow pan. Freeze. Remove from freezer about an hour before serving and break up into slush. Pour into punch bowl and add carbonated lemon-lime beverage. Makes 18 half-cup servings.

Note: Frozen slush can be kept in freezer up to three months.

LION HOUSE

Sunshine Citrus Punch

1 6-ounce can frozen
    lemonade concentrate
1 6-ounce can frozen grape-
    fruit juice concentrate
1 6-ounce can frozen
    pineapple juice concen-
    trate
2 cups water
3½ cups club soda, chilled
3½ cups ginger ale, chilled

COMBINE LEMONADE CONCENTRATE, grapefruit juice concentrate, and pineapple juice concentrate with water in a large non-metal pitcher or punch bowl. Chill in refrigerator. Just before serving, add club soda and ginger ale. Stir to blend. Garnish punch bowl with fresh fruit slices or ice ring, if desired. Makes 25 half-cup servings.

LION HOUSE

Cranberry Punch

1 quart cranberry juice
    cocktail
1 quart apple juice
1 quart sugar-free
    carbonated lemon-
    lime beverage

IN A LARGE NONMETAL PITCHER, stir together cranberry and apple juices. Cover and chill. Just before serving, add lemon-lime beverage and stir gently. Makes 24 half-cup servings.

LION HOUSE

Santa Claus Punch

2 packages unsweetened
    raspberry punch powder
1 cup sugar
4 cups cranberry juice cock-
    tail
12 cups (3 quarts) crushed
    ice and water

IN A LARGE PITCHER COMBINE punch mix with sugar. Add cranberry juice and stir till dissolved. Mix in crushed ice and water. Makes 32 half-cup servings.

LION HOUSE

Apricot Refresher

1 cup orange juice, chilled
1 46-ounce can apricot
    nectar, chilled
1 6-ounce can frozen
    lemonade concentrate
3½ cups club soda, chilled
1 quart pineapple sherbet

COMBINE ORANGE JUICE, APRICOT nectar, and lemonade concentrate in a large nonmetal punch bowl; mix well. Refrigerate if desired. Just before serving, gently stir in club soda and scoops of sherbet. Makes 32 half-cup servings.

LION HOUSE

Apricot Nectar Shake

1 cup chilled apricot nectar

2 teaspoons lemon juice

Pinch salt

1 cup vanilla ice milk

Blend apricot nectar with lemon juice and salt in blender. Add ice milk and blend to desired consistency. Serve immediately. Makes 4 servings.

Lion House

Pictured on page 159.

Fruit Punch with Sherbet

2 large cans (46 ounces each) pineapple-grapefruit juice

1 6-ounce can frozen lemon juice

1 6-ounce can frozen lime juice

2 cans water

2 shakes salt

1 quart lime sherbet

2 quarts ginger ale

In a large nonmetal pitcher, mix fruit juices, water, and salt, and let stand overnight in refrigerator. Before serving, add lime sherbet and ginger ale. Makes 30 punch-cup servings.

Lion House

Specialty
Drinks

APRICOT NECTAR SHAKE.
RECIPE ON PAGE 158.

Banana Freeze

4 cups sugar

6 cups water

5 oranges

2 lemons

5 bananas

1 quart apricot or pineapple
juice

½ to 1 large (2-liter) bottle
lemon-lime soda

IN A LARGE SAUCEPAN BOIL THE sugar and water three to five minutes, until sugar is well dissolved. Cool. In a large bowl squeeze the juice from the oranges and lemons. Mash the bananas. Combine the orange and lemon juices, mashed bananas, and apricot or pineapple juice. Add to sugar and water mixture and freeze in large pan. When ready to serve, chop and spoon into sherbet dishes or punch cups and pour lemon-lime carbonated beverage over it.

LION HOUSE

Frosty Frappe for a Crowd

1 gallon pineapple sherbet

3 10-ounce packages frozen
raspberries

1½ cups frozen blueberries

1½ cups frozen boysen-
berries

4 or 5 bananas, peeled and
mashed

½ to 1 large (2-liter) bottle
lemon-lime soda

SOFTEN SHERBET AND PARTIALLY THAW raspberries, blueberries, and boysenberries. Spoon sherbet into large serving bowl. Add partially thawed fruits and mashed bananas and stir just till blended. Stir in carbonated lemon-lime beverage a little at a time to keep slushy consistency. Serve immediately by spooning into punch cups. Makes 32 servings.

LION HOUSE

Pictured on page 148.

Grenadine Freeze

1 cup sugar
2 cups water
2 cups grapefruit juice
½ cup grenadine syrup
1 tablespoon lemon juice
1 16-ounce bottle lemon-
    lime carbonated
    beverage
1 thinly sliced lemon
Maraschino cherries

In a large saucepan boil sugar and water together. Stir until sugar is dissolved. Remove from heat. Add grapefruit juice, grenadine syrup, and lemon juice. Pour into shallow pan and freeze. To serve, chop frozen mixture and place into serving cups. Pour lemon-lime beverage over top and garnish with lemon slice and maraschino cherry. Makes 14 half-cup servings.

Lion House

Raspberry Slush for a Crowd

3 packets unsweetened rasp-
    berry punch powder
4 cups sugar
4 cups warm water
1 46-ounce can pineapple
    juice
1 12-ounce can frozen
    lemonade
1 6-ounce can frozen lemon
    juice
3 10-ounce packages frozen
    raspberries
3½ quarts water
1 2-liter bottle carbonated
    lemon-lime beverage

In a 2-gallon container, dissolve raspberry punch mix and sugar in warm water. Add pineapple juice, lemonade, lemon juice, and raspberries and enough water (about 3½ quarts) to make 2 gallons. Stir till blended. Pour into large freezer containers and freeze. When ready to serve, thaw till slushy. Pour into punch bowl or individual punch cups and add carbonated lemon-lime beverage. Makes 75 half-cup servings.

Lion House

Fruit Freeze

2 16-ounce cans grapefruit
    segments, undrained
1 11-ounce can mandarin
    oranges, undrained
½ cup sugar
1 small jar maraschino
    cherries, undrained
1 20-ounce can crushed
    pineapple, undrained
1 12-ounce bottle lemon-
    lime carbonated
    beverage
1 pint lime sherbet

WHIRL GRAPEFRUIT SECTIONS, ORANGES, and sugar together in blender for about 30 seconds. Chop cherries. Add cherries, cherry juice, and crushed pineapple to blended fruits. Pour into freezer trays or loaf pans and freeze. When ready to serve, chop frozen mixture and spoon into serving cups. Pour lemon-lime beverage over top and add a small scoop of sherbet. Makes 15 to 20 punch-cup servings.

LION HOUSE

Three-Fruit Slush

1 cup sugar
2 cups water
2 cups mashed bananas
½ cup fresh lemon juice
1 6-ounce can frozen
    lemonade, no water
    added
1 6-ounce can frozen orange
    juice, 3 cans water added
1 2-liter bottle ginger ale
    (optional)

COMBINE SUGAR AND WATER IN A medium saucepan, and boil together about 3 minutes. Cool. Mash bananas. Add bananas and fruit juices to sugar syrup. Pour into pans for freezing; freeze until slushy. Stir occasionally. Remove from pans and beat with an egg beater once during freezing, if desired. Serve slush plain or pour ginger ale or similar carbonated beverage over slush just before serving. Makes about 20 half-cup servings.

LION HOUSE

Index

Numbers in boldface type indicate photographs.